SALAMANCA 1812

SALAMANCA 1812

TEXT BY
IAN FLETCHER

BATTLESCENES BY
BILL YOUNGHUSBAND

First published in Great Britain in 1997 by Osprey Publishing,
Elms Court, Chapel Way, Botley, Oxford OX2 9LP, United Kingdom.
Email: info@ospreypublishing.com

Also published as Campaign 48: *Salamanca 1812*

ISBN 1 84176 277 6

Military Editor: Sharon van der Merwe
Design: The Black Spot

Colour bird's eye view illustrations by Peter Harper
Cartography by Micromap
Back cover map by The Map Studio

Tourist information by Martin Marix Evans

Index by Alan Rutter

Battlescene artwork by Bill Younghusband
Filmset in Singapore by Pica Ltd.
Printed in China through World Print Ltd.

01 02 03 04 05 10 9 8 7 6 5 4 3 2 1

FOR A CATALOGUE OF ALL BOOKS PUBLISHED BY OSPREY MILITARY AND AVIATION
PLEASE WRITE TO:

The Marketing Manager, Osprey Direct UK,
PO Box 140, Wellingborough, Northants,
NN8 4ZA, United Kingdom.
Email: info@ospreydirect.co.uk

The Marketing Manager, Osprey Direct USA,
c/o Motorbooks International, PO Box 1, Osceola,
WI 54020-0001, USA.
Email: info@ospreydirectusa.com

www.ospreypublishing.com

KEY TO MILITARY SYMBOLS

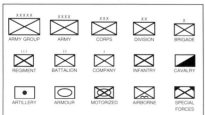

Acknowledgements

Thanks to Ian Hook, Curator of the Essex Regimental Museum,
Chelmsford, for allowing me to photograph the captured 'eagle' of
the 62nd Ligne; to Richard Old, for the use of several important
works on the campaign and with whom I spent many days (and
nights!) following the Salamanca campaign trail from the Douro to
the Tormes; to Tim Edwards, for access to his superb weapons col-
lection; to Philip Haythornthwaite for his usual kind assistance; and
to Julie, Jeremy, Paul and Tony of the Midas Battlefield Tours
Exploring Officers' Club, with whom I spent many a most enjoyable
day at Salamanca in September 1996. Thanks.

Artist's note

FRONT COVER: **Portrait of Wellington and Sir William Carr
Beresford at Salamanca 1812. (© The Art Archive)**

PAGE 2 **Royal Horse Artillery teams coming into action in
the Peninsula.**

TITLE PAGE **Imperial Eagle of the French 62nd Regiment,
captured by Lieutenant Pearce of the 44th (East Essex)
Regiment.**

CONTENTS

ACTIONS IN THE PENINSULA 1811

BAY OF BISCAY

FRANCE • Toulouse • Béziers

• Coruña • El Ferrol • Gijón • Santander • San Sebastián • Bayonne • Carcassonne • Narbonne

Santiago de Compostela • Oviedo ASTURIAS • Bilbao • Lourdes • Perpignan

GALICIA • Lugo • Vittoria • Sorauren ANDORRA

• Vigo • Orense • León • Astorga Esla • Burgos • Logroño Arga Pamplona PYRENEES • Gerona

• Braga • Benavente LEÓN • Soria Ebro • Saragossa • Lérida CATALONIA

• Oporto Douro • Zamora • Toro • Valladolid Duero • Barcelona

PORTUGAL Almeida Salamanca • Alba de Tormes SPAIN ARAGON • Tortosa • Tarragona

Busaco • Guarda Ciudad Rodrigo Fuentes de Oñoro Guadalajara MALLORCA

The French garrison at Ciudad Rodrigo numbers 5,000

Joseph's garrison at Madrid about 15,000 troops • Teruel • Castellón de la Plana

5 May 1811: British victory at Fuentes de Oñoro Madrid • Cuenca Turia

Castelo Branco Almaraz • Talavera • Aranjuez Júcar VALENCIA IBIZA

Rolíça Cáceres • Trujillo • Toledo NEW CASTILE • Valencia

Having captured the key border fortresses of Ciudad Rodrigo and Almeida, Massena moves toward Lisbon. He is forced to pull back due to lack of provisions in March 1811, pursued by Wellington

May–June 1811: Beresford's attempts to take Badajoz fail

Vimeiro Torres Vedras Elvas Badajoz Guadiana • Ciudad Real • Albacete

Lisbon • Setúbal Albuera ESTREMADURA • Alicante

16 May 1811: Beresford forced to march south to fight Soult at Albuera. Soult beaten and his attempt to relieve the Badajoz garrison fails

• Évora • Baylen • Murcia

• Beja Guadiana • Córdoba **Soult spends most of the year campaigning in Andalusia** MURCIA • Cartagena

Guadalquivir • Jaén • Lorca

• Huelva • Seville ANDALUSIA • Granada MEDITERRANEAN SEA

1811 ends with the French occupying most of the Peninsula with some 350,000 troops. Napoleon has begun to withdraw thousands of troops for the Russian campaign. Wellington's Anglo-Portuguese army numbers some 60,000 of whom a third are Portuguese. 1812 begins with Wellington on the Portuguese border, poised to strike at Ciudad Rodrigo

Genil GRANADA • Almería

5 March 1811: The French force besieging Cadiz defeated at Barossa

• Cádiz Barrosa • Malaga Chélif

• Gibraltar N

• Tangier • Tétouan • Oran

• Melilla

■ Garrison town

0 — 100 Miles

0 — 200 Km

INTRODUCTION

BELOW, LEFT **The Battle of Corunna, 16 January 1809. Sir John Moore is carried from the field after being mortally wounded by an enemy cannonball. Moore's efforts during the harrowing Corunna campaign ensured that the British army was able to re-embark and return to England in relative safety, even though it cost him his life. (After a print by Durpray)**

BELOW **An incident during the battle of Vimeiro, 21 August 1808. Although it was fought four days after the battle of Roliça, this was Wellesley's first important victory in the Peninsula and one which brought his name to the fore throughout Europe.**

On 22 July 1808, HMS *Crocodile* nudged its way into the port of Corunna in northern Spain, with Lt. Gen. Sir Arthur Wellesley on board. Wellesley had sailed to Spain as commander of a 14,000-strong British force with the intention of supporting the people of both Portugal and Spain who had risen up against the invading French armies. Unfortunately, Wellesley was told in no uncertain terms by the local Spanish Junta that his presence, and that of his army, was not welcome, and he was advised to continue his journey along the coast of Portugal and seek help there. Wellesley departed Corunna on 24 July. Four years later – almost to the day – Sir Arthur, by then Lord Wellington, achieved one of his greatest successes on the field of battle when he defeated the French Army of Portugal under Marshal Marmont at the battle of Salamanca.

The road to Salamanca involved four years of hard slog for Wellington, who had to contend not only with numerically superior enemy forces, but with an anxious British government, worried lest its only army perished on the dusty Iberian plains. Added to this was the so-called 'croaking', the whispering campaign conducted by some of Wellington's own officers who saw little prospect of success, and who advocated evacuating the Peninsula as soon as possible. This campaign

The crossing of the Douro, 12 May 1809. Following his return to the Peninsula, after having been acquitted of all charges arising from the Convention of Cintra, Wellesley drove Soult from Portugal in a daring operation which involved his men crossing the Douro beneath the very noses of the French, suffering very few casualties in the process. (After a painting by Simkin)

reached its height during the spring and summer of 1810, although by the spring of 1811, when Massena's starving French army had been forced from Portugal following its disastrous sojourn in front of the impenetrable Lines of Torres Vedras, even the 'croakers' could see some light at the end of the tunnel.

The British army's campaign in the Peninsula began in August 1808 with a landing at the mouth of the Mondego River at Figueras. On 16 August the army fought its first action, near an old mill at Brillos, and suffered its first casualty of the war, Lt. Bunbury, of the 95th Rifles. The following day Wellesley's army fought and won its first battle, at Roliça, although by later standards this was really nothing more than a large skirmish. On 21 August Wellesley defeated Delaborde at Vimeiro, his first major victory, and a battle which gave a clear indication how victory in the Peninsula was to be achieved. The dense French columns crumbled before the superior firepower of the British line, aided and abetted by Wellesley's skilful choice of position and by the efficient use of his limited artillery. Sadly, and perhaps more ominous, was the behaviour of the British cavalry, on this occasion the 20th Light Dragoons, who performed the first of a series of ill-managed charges, something which was to continue right up until Waterloo some seven years later. But if the victory at Vimeiro ushered in the beginning of a long series of triumphs of the British line, it also marked one of the most controversial incidents of the Peninsular War, the notorious Convention of Cintra.

The convention was signed following an armistice, agreed between Wellesley and Gen. Kellerman, representing Junot's French army. Prior to the signing of the convention, Wellesley had been superseded by two senior generals, Sir Hew Dalrymple and Sir Harry Burrard, who had

arrived from England, while a third, Sir John Moore, was also on his way to Portugal. Under the terms of the convention, the defeated French army was allowed to sail back to France in British ships with all of its accumulated plunder as well as its arms. Naturally, this outraged the people in Britain and Wellesley, Dalrymple and Burrard were recalled to England to face a Court of Inquiry.

Meanwhile, the British army was driven from Spain by Marshal Soult who, on 16 January 1809, had fought the battle of Corunna against a British army under Sir John Moore. The resulting British victory allowed the army to embark in relative safety, although it cost Moore his life. The retreat to Corunna was also one of the more harrowing episodes of the war, as the discipline of many British units vanished amid the snows of the bleak Galician mountains. The episode was to be repeated in November 1812 during the retreat from Burgos, which was said by many to have been the more terrible of the two.

Wellesley was acquitted of his part in the Convention of Cintra and he returned to Portugal on 22 April 1809, when his ship, HMS *Surveillante*, sailed into Lisbon. Within just three weeks he had formulated his strategy for ejecting the French from Portugal and on 12 May, in one of the most daring operations of the war, his men crossed the River Douro and drove Soult's men from the city of Oporto. By the end of the month Portugal was clear of the so-called Army of Portugal. From Oporto, Wellesley turned south to link up with the Spaniards under the ageing Gen. Cuesta, although the alliance between the two men was not one of the most productive. The Spaniards failed to make good their promises of supplies or, more importantly, transport. Moreover, Cuesta was loathe to take orders from Wellesley, whom, somewhat ironically, he regarded as an English heretic. The two men, however, did manage a

The 48th Regiment in action during the battle of Talavera, 27-28 July 1809. The battle was Wellesley's first in Spain following his return to the Peninsula in April 1809. (After a painting by Simkin)

degree of co-operation and by the summer of 1809 had concentrated their forces at Talavera. Here, on 27-28 July, with little or no help from his Spanish allies, Wellesley achieved one of his most hard-fought victories beneath the blazing Spanish sun. The two-day battle cost him some 5,000 casualties against 7,500 French, but it did earn him the title of Lord Wellington, Marquis of Talavera, a name first used by him when, on 27 September 1809, he signed himself 'Wellington'.

The battle of Talavera ushered in a period of inactivity which was to continue until September 1810. During this 14-month period his army watched and waited on the Spanish–Portuguese border as Massena's forces gathered in preparation for the invasion of Portugal. It was during this period that Wellington had to deal with the unease which was rife throughout his camp. Even senior commanders such as Robert Craufurd, whose Light Division found itself at the sharp end of operations on the border during the summer of 1810, saw little cause for optimism and was one of the 'croakers' Wellington complained of.

THE LINES OF TORRES VEDRAS

While Wellington's army lingered, sometimes uneasily on the border, his engineers were busy supervising one of their commander's great masterstrokes, the construction of the Lines of Torres Vedras. These three lines of fortification, with a fourth close to Lisbon itself, formed a series of barriers, both natural and man-made, which stretched across the 30-

mile wide Lisbon peninsula. They dammed rivers and streams, constructed forts on hilltops, destroyed roads and constructed a variety of obstacles to make penetration by the French virtually impossible. A 'scorched earth' policy was carried out, as crops were either destroyed or absorbed into the Lines, while the population itself was resettled, leaving scores of villages and hamlets deserted. Wellington was absolutely determined that the French army would gain nothing from the land in front of his lines.

The retreat to the Lines of Torres Vedras began in August 1810, and Wellington stopped only once, at the immensely strong position atop the ridge at Busaco, to turn and fight what was really just a delaying action. Massena's divisions attacked Wellington on 27 September, but met with little success as his men were driven helter-skelter back down the very steep slopes which they had struggled up in vain. The victory was one of Wellington's finest, and saw his Portuguese troops establish themselves with their previously unconvinced British allies. On the morning after the battle, however, Massena's cavalry discovered a road which outflanked Wellington's position to the north, and the respite for which Wellington had hoped was cut short.

A few days after Busaco Wellington's men began to enter the Lines. None of the forts were manned by Wellington's regulars, which was an unusual system of defence. Regular soldiers were to be used as a mobile force to counter any possible breakthrough by Massena, and the forts themselves were guarded by Portuguese militia and British seamen.

BELOW **The battle of Fuentes de Onoro, 3-5 May 1811. This was Massena's last battle in the Peninsula as he was recalled to Paris shortly afterwards. The battle, ostensibly an attempt by Massena to relieve the garrison of Almeida, ended in a hard-won victory for Wellington although he later said it was turned into a defeat when Brennier, the governor of Almeida, and his garrison made good their escape beneath the eyes of the careless blockading British troops a few days later. (After a print by Thomas St. Clair)**

Wellington's fears were unfounded, however. When Massena arrived in front of the Lines, he looked up in surprise at what proved to be an impregnable position: the construction of the Lines had been effected in great secrecy. Ironically, reports from Royal Engineer officers who had been sent back to the Lines by Wellington's chief engineer, Sir Richard Fletcher, suggest that they themselves had little faith in them, adding that the Portuguese troops would run at the sound of the first shot fired. Fortunately, this pessimism was misplaced and the Lines of Torres Vedras proved to be as successful as Wellington had hoped.

Apart from a brief half-hearted attempt to attack the Lines at Sobral, Massena merely settled down in front of them to wait, for what we are not sure. In November 1810, faced with starvation, he pulled his army back towards Santarem in the hope that enough food could be found to sustain his troops. It was a futile hope, however, and in March 1811 he was finally forced to concede defeat and began his retreat north in the direction of Coimbra. There followed a number of fights – at Pombal, Redinha, Condeixa, Casal Nova and, notably, Foz d'Arouce – as Wellington harried Massena's rearguard all the way to the Portuguese border. The last action of the retreat came on 3 April 1811 at Sabugal, until finally, Wellington drove Massena back over the border and into Spain.

On 3-5 May 1811 Wellington engaged and thwarted Massena at Fuentes de Onoro. The battle was an attempt by Massena to relieve the beleaguered garrison of Almeida, and was the last to be fought by the

ABOVE **The 7th (Royal Fusiliers) make their attack during the closing stages of the battle of Albuera, 16 May 1811. It was one of the bloodiest battles of the war and was also one where Wellington was not present, the army on this occasion being commanded, somewhat controversially, by William Carr Beresford. (After a painting by Wollen)**

RIGHT **The storming of Ciudad Rodrigo, 19 January 1812, after a painting by Harry Payne. Many anachronisms appear, such as Belgic shakos, which were not worn, but otherwise a good representation of the attack. The ladders are also somewhat sturdier than the actual ones used. Indeed, many of the ladders were apparently made from chopped up wagons.**

ABOVE **The storming of Badajoz, 6 April 1812, after a painting by Atkinson. The Light Division are seen mounting one of over 40 separate attacks which were delivered against the breaches but without success. The town eventually fell after the two diversionary attacks, at the castle and at the San Vincente bastions, succeeded.**

veteran French marshal as he was replaced by Marmont a few weeks later. Just 11 days later one of the bloodiest battles of the Peninsular War was fought at Albuera. Wellington took no part in the battle; the Allied army under Beresford was laying siege to the fortress of Badajoz and they abandoned this to meet Soult's troops. The victory at Albuera was due almost entirely to the stubborn British infantry who refused to buckle in the face of a tremendous French onslaught. Severe British casualties were the price of this heroism, however, in a battle which later provoked much argument and bitterness as Beresford defended himself against widespread criticism of his command.

There were a number of minor engagements and manoeuvring and counter-manoeuvring by both armies until

THE AFTERMATH OF BADAJOZ
Following the storming of Badajoz on the night of 6/7 April 1812 Wellington's men went beserk and sacked the town in an orgy of violence. When Phillipon and his garrison chose to fight on despite the fact that the walls had been breached they waived all rights to mercy. Strangely enough, they escaped relatively unscathed afterwards when Wellington's men turned on the inhabitants instead and the shocking scenes that followed the storming have gone down in legend as some of the most disgraceful in the history of the British army. The sacking of the town lasted for a full 72 hours and, as Napier wrote, 'the tumult rather subsided than was quelled'.

December 1811, when Wellington was ready to begin the siege of Ciudad Rodrigo, the French-held fortress guarding the northern corridor between Spain and Portugal. After a siege of just 11 days, Allied troops stormed the town on 19 January 1812, although at some cost. Henry Mackinnon, leading the 3rd Division's assault on the Great Breach, was killed and Robert Craufurd, commander of the Light Division, mortally wounded. The loss of Craufurd, who died on 23 January, was perhaps the greatest blow suffered by Wellington during the war. The storming of Ciudad Rodrigo was significant in that it was the first time Wellington's army had taken a town by storm - the historian Sir John Fortescue goes so far as to state that it was the first time a British army had successfully stormed a European fortress. Little was done to maintain order afterwards, and a degree of plunder and misbehaviour occurred before discipline was restored. At Ciudad Rodrigo Wellington's men got a taste of what could be expected in the event of a successful assault, a taste which they enjoyed to the full ten weeks later at Badajoz.

With Ciudad Rodrigo in his hands, Wellington turned his attention to the mighty fortress of Badajoz, guarding the southern route between the two Iberian nations. The French garrison, commanded by the very able Baron Armand Phillipon, sat back confidently behind huge walls, 46 feet high in places, and awaited the British assault. Once again, Wellington's men toiled in extreme conditions of rain and biting wind, with poor tools and regularly shelled by the French. When the assault finally came on the night of 6 April, the fury of the attack was met with equal violence by the defenders who employed every conceivable means to keep their assailants from gaining the breaches. Despite hurling themselves at the breaches over 40 times, the British and Portuguese attackers made little headway. Two diversionary attacks, both by means of escalade, finally ensured the town's capture. The fall of Badajoz was followed by 72 hours of drunken debauchery as the triumphant soldiers, driven to the point of madness by the assault, sacked the place from top to bottom.

Wellington's army staggered from Badajoz on 9 April and made its way back north to Ciudad Rodrigo which was being threatened by Marmont. The threat failed to materialise, however, and Wellington was able to stop and lay plans for the campaign that would, he hoped, see the Allies in Madrid that same summer. He was to be proved correct, of course, but first he would have to fight one of the most decisive battles of his career, Salamanca.

OPPOSING PLANS

With both Ciudad Rodrigo and Badajoz in his hands, Wellington could feel more secure as he began to plan his thrust into Spain. There were two options open to him: an advance south into Estremadura against the army of Marshal Soult, or a move east against Marshal Marmont commanding the Army of Portugal in central Spain. A move against Soult would certainly be the more appealing as far as the Spaniards were concerned. After all, the Supreme Junta of Spain had long since been in Cadiz and it would not take too much effort to relieve the city. From a military standpoint, however, it offered few advantages. Advancing south would simply prompt Soult into moving north where he would easily be able to join forces with either Marmont or Suchet, who was occupied on the eastern coast of Spain. An advance against Marmont, on the other hand, would represent a serious threat to French communications with France. This move would probably induce the French to bring more forces to support Marmont but Wellington planned to prevent this with a number of counter-measures. Spanish

British cavalry on patrol in the Peninsula. The Allies enjoyed the advantage of having the local population, and in particular the clergy, on their side in the Peninsula, both of whom were a great source of intelligence.

French infantry in the firing line, 1812. A veteran sergeant steadies his men whilst an officer stands coolly behind him.

guerrillas were employed to prevent French units from concentrating, diversionary tactics were used on the eastern coast to distract those French forces, while in Andalucia the Spanish commander Ballasteros was ordered to make preparations for an offensive from the south to keep Soult occupied. Elsewhere in the Peninsula, from the Mediterranean to the Bay of Biscay, Spanish guerrillas and Portuguese militia were given orders to harry and hustle the French whenever possible.

While Wellington ensured that all his main lines of communication were improved and repaired from the ports of Lisbon and Oporto to the Spanish border, he planned to sever the links between Soult's army south of the River Tagus and Marmont's forces north of the river. This involved a daring raid on the bridge of boats and the forts over the Tagus at Almaraz. A force of 10,000 British and Portuguese infantry, commanded by Rowland Hill and supported by a battery of heavy guns, raided Almaraz on 12 May 1812. 'Daddy' Hill, as he was known by his men, was probably the only commander trusted enough by Wellington to carry out such as raid, and he did not disappoint his commander-in-chief. In fact, Hill had already demonstrated his ability in an independent command when he attacked and routed a French force at the village of Arroyo dos Molinos in October 1811. The operation against the bridge at Almaraz was carried out with similar élan, his infantry, notably the 50th and 71st

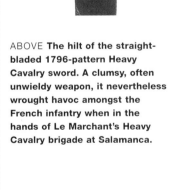

Regiments, storming the fort on the southern bank of the Tagus before driving the French defenders back over the bridge of boats. With the French in full retreat, Hill destroyed the bridge and forts and thus severed direct communications between Soult and Marmont.

The destruction at Almaraz was a major inconvenience for the French, but Wellington still had to contend with five French armies in Spain. Early in 1812 some 27,000 troops had been removed from the armies of Suchet, Dorsenne, Marmont, Soult and Joseph for service in the army Napoleon was preparing for the invasion of Russia. Other battalions were sent south to replace them, but they were not of the same quality, nor were they as numerous. However, the French armies still numbered some 230,000 men, against which Wellington had just over 60,000. Wellington had several advantages over his French adversaries, the most significant being the co-operation of the Spanish people, a vital factor that was to prove crucial in his campaign in the Peninsula.

ABOVE **The hilt of the straight-bladed 1796-pattern Heavy Cavalry sword. A clumsy, often unwieldy weapon, it nevertheless wrought havoc amongst the French infantry when in the hands of Le Marchant's Heavy Cavalry brigade at Salamanca.**

RIGHT **The superb 1796-pattern Light Cavalry sabre, as designed by John Gaspard Le Marchant, killed tragically at Salamanca.**

Wellington later acknowledged the importance of the Spanish guerrillas in his final victory, and indeed, it is difficult to imagine him achieving it without them. Spain is a vast country, and the French simply could not concentrate enough men to seriously affect Wellington's position. They may have had an opportunity earlier in the war when Wellington was struggling against both political and military odds to establish himself in the Peninsula, but by 1812, those days were long gone. Wellington had realised early on the vital necessity of co-operating with the Spanish and Portuguese people and by the summer of 1812 he had begun to exert his influence over both the Spanish generals and guerrillas. The stress he placed on having the co-operation of the local people can be gauged by the fact that, when he invaded southern France in the winter of 1813-14, he sent home several thousand Spanish troops who had begun to exact their own revenge on French towns and villages. This may have left him short of men, but he could not risk the sort of resistance movement in France that had played havoc with the French during their occupation of Spain.

The guerrillas had an equally important part to play in Wellington's intelligence system. It was, of course, vital to know what was happening 'on the other side of the hill', and in this respect the French suffered badly. They undoubtedly had their own network of spies, but the information gleaned from it was trifling when compared to that run by Wellington. In George Scovell, he had an officer who was a master of decoding enemy ciphers, while his own group of 'corre spondents' kept him regularly informed of French troop movements and numbers. Dr Patrick Curtis, Regius Professor of the Irish College in Salamanca, was probably the best-known of these, and supplied Wellington with a great deal of information prior to the Salamanca campaign. Indeed, Curtis dined with Marmont himself on several occasions, and although suspected by some French officers, was never caught and convicted of spying. The Spanish guerrillas, meanwhile, saw to it that Wellington received as much information as was asked for, while enemy despatches were brought in regularly, often stained with the blood of their former bearers. This was in stark contrast to Marmont's intelligence system, which relied as much upon the torturing of local people as it did upon the stealth of French officers.

The advantages that Wellington gained through his co-operation with the Spanish guerrillas was therefore of great importance, and despite the numerical superiority of his adversaries he was able to take to the field in the early summer of 1812 full of confidence. Diversionary operations in Andalucia, along the Bay of Biscay and on the eastern coast of Spain were put into operation while Rowland Hill, with some 18,000 regulars, guarded the southern route between the two Iberian countries at Badajoz and Elvas. All was now ready and, on 13 June 1812, Wellington and his army, 48,000 men with 54 guns, crossed the River Agueda to begin their march east. It was the beginning of a momentous eight weeks that took them from the Portuguese border to the Spanish capital, Madrid.

The hilt of the 1796-pattern infantry officer's sword, carried by the majority of Wellington's officers at Salamanca.

THE CAMPAIGN

On the morning of 17 June, four days after his advance began, Wellington reached Salamanca. There was little or no resistance and his men began filing into the town the same morning. Marmont, in fact, had withdrawn his army to a position 20 miles north of the town, between Bleines and Fuente Sauco. He had, however, left behind a garrison of 800 men to man three forts in the town, the San Vincente, La Merced and the San Gaetano.

These forts were situated in the south-east of the town, high above the River Tormes. San Vincente was the strongest, boasting some 30 guns. The fort of La Merced mounted only two guns but they dominated the old Roman bridge into the town and were a source of no little annoyance to Wellington's men. On the basis of reports and sketches provided by his Spanish agents, Wellington believed the forts to be relatively weak and apparently went to Salamanca expecting to face three fortified convents. However, they proved to be much stronger owing to the large amount of stone – hewn from the colleges and buildings that once stood on the same ground – with which the French engineers had been able to strengthen them. The ground upon which the buildings had stood had thus been cleared, and provided a first-class field of fire for the garrison. Moreover, the San Vincente could only be approached across the open ground as it was protected to the south by a cliff, at the bottom of which ran the River Tormes, and to the east by a deep ravine. Matters were not helped either by the usual lack of a decent Allied siege train, something that would plague them at Burgos three months later. Indeed, there were only four 18-pdrs. available to Clinton for the reduction of the forts, although six other heavy guns were on their way to Salamanca. And so, while Wellington and the bulk of his army took themselves off to a position at San Cristobal, three miles north of Salamanca, Clinton and his 6th Division stayed behind in the town to lay siege to the three forts.

THE SIEGE OF THE SALAMANCA FORTS

The siege of the Salamanca forts began on the night of 17 June, but it was to be a full ten days before the garrisons finally capitulated. Clinton's 6th Division had little experience of siege warfare, although even Wellington's veterans, the 3rd, 4th, 5th and Light Divisions, would probably have struggled to deal with the situation. The rubble and debris scattered round, combined with the old, very solid foundations of the buildings previously on the site, made entrenching very difficult, although the Allied riflemen made good use of the debris as cover from which to snipe at the French defenders. The unsatisfactory siege dragged on until the evening of 23 June, when 350 men from Hulse's and Bowes'

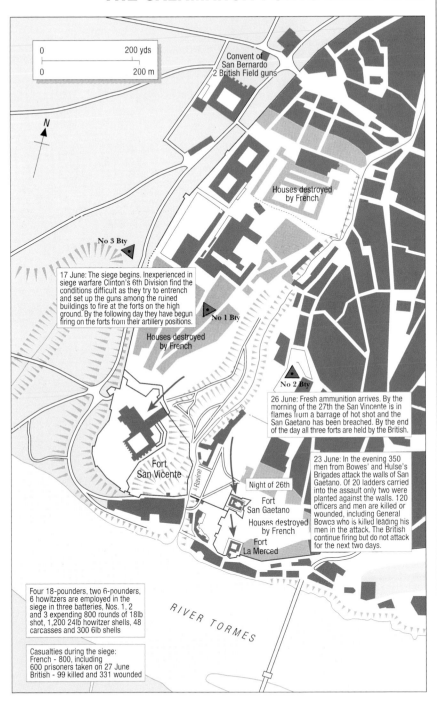

0   200 yds

0   200 m

Convent of
San Bernardo
2 British Field guns

Houses destroyed
by French

N

No 3 Bty

17 June: The siege begins. Inexperienced in siege warfare Clinton's 6th Division find the conditions difficult as they try to entrench and set up the guns among the ruined buildings to fire at the forts on the high ground. By the following day they have begun firing on the forts from their artillery positions.

No 1 Bty

Houses destroyed
by French

No 2 Bty

26 June: Fresh ammunition arrives. By the morning of the 27th the San Vincente is in flames from a barrage of hot shot and the San Gaetano has been breached. By the end of the day all three forts are held by the British.

Fort
San Vicente

Ravine

Night of 26th

23 June: In the evening 350 men from Bowes' and Hulse's Brigades attack the walls of San Gaetano. Of 20 ladders carried into the assault only two were planted against the walls. 120 officers and men are killed or wounded, including General Bowes who is killed leading his men in the attack. The British continue firing but do not attack for the next two days.

Fort
San Gaetano

Houses destroyed
by French

Fort
La Merced

Four 18-pounders, two 6-pounders, 6 howitzers are employed in the siege in three batteries, Nos. 1, 2 and 3 expending 800 rounds of 18lb shot, 1,200 24lb howitzer shells, 48 carcasses and 300 6lb shells

Casualties during the siege:
French - 800, including
600 prisoners taken on 27 June
British - 99 killed and 331 wounded

RIVER TORMES

brigades of the 6th Division were thrown against the walls of the San Gaetano fort in a futile attempt to escalade it. Of the 20 ladders carried into the assault, only two were actually planted against the walls at a cost of some 120 officers and men who were either killed or wounded. Among the dead was Gen. Bowes who had insisted on joining his men in the attack. Bowes was wounded early on, but after being patched up, returned to lead his men and was fatally wounded.

The view from Wellington's position on 20-22 June at San Cristobal, three miles north of Salamanca. Marmont's numerically inferior army deployed on the plain in the distance, causing Wellington to remark, 'It's damned tempting. I've a good mind to attack 'em.'

Despite the setback, fresh supplies of ammunition arrived on 26 June. By the morning of 27 June the San Vincente was in flames from a barrage of hot shot, while a practicable breach had been made in the San Gaetano; at the end of the day all three forts were in Allied hands. Some 600 unwounded Frenchmen thus marched out of the forts and into captivity while Wellington was left to reflect upon the 430-strong casualty list which had been the cost of this frustrating ten-day episode.

While the siege of the Salamanca forts was in progress there had been much marching and counter-marching by both armies during a period which has become one of the memorable features of the Salamanca campaign. Having left Clinton's 6th Division in Salamanca, Wellington's main army had marched north to the heights above San Cristobal, three miles outside the town, on 19 June. This position was a strong one, giving Wellington a long, sloping, commanding height with a concealed reverse slope – his trademark position and stretched from the village of San Cristobal itself as far as the River Tormes at Cabrerizos, on which rested his right flank.

The Fall of the Forts

The following day Marmont arrived in front of San Cristobal, intent on relieving the forts in Salamanca. From his position upon the heights above the village Wellington gazed out over the vast plain before him as Marmont's force, some 25,000 men, manoeuvred. In fact, Marmont had with him all of his force, save for Bonnet's division which was still in the Asturias. The French advanced and soon were just 800 yards from the Allied position, prompting an outbreak of cannon-fire from British guns as if to warn off their adversaries. The French reply was as much in defiance as it was an attempt to serve as a signal to the beleaguered garrisons of the Salamanca forts. There was little direct action on 20 June, although French troops did attack the village of Moriscos, situated under the Allied right centre, which was held by the 68th Light Infantry. Despite a sharp attack on the village the 68th held firm until nightfall when Wellington ordered them to fall back, having suffered 50 casualties.

Wellington welcomed the French attack and hoped that Marmont would follow it up the next day. Indeed, at dusk he stood in full view of the French gunners, issuing orders to his generals and giving them detailed instructions as to their role on the following day. This impromptu meeting was cut short, however, when a few shots came bouncing in among them, prompting a prudent withdrawal. A serious attack by the French against a numerically superior force – Wellington outnumbered Marmont by 8,000 men – occupying a strong position would have been dangerous to say the least. Moreover, in the event of failure, which would almost certainly have been the outcome, the plain behind Marmont offered little in the way of protection. Certainly, there was no feature similar to the wood that was to save him from total destruction a month later at Salamanca.

Unfortunately for Wellington, Marmont did nothing on 21 June other than ride forward to reconnoitre Wellington's position. There was some skirmishing on the Allied right flank, but the day was one of inactivity with both sides remaining within cannon-shot of each other without doing any harm. Wellington was up well before dawn on 22 June and soon realised that Marmont was not about to attack him. He decided to draw him into a battle instead and, at 7am, Wellington ordered the 51st and 68th, along with the skirmishers from the Light Brigade of the King's German Legion, to attack the French piquets upon a knoll above the village of Moriscos. In the event of a strong French counterattack, Sir Thomas Graham was to support these troops with the whole of the 1st

The church at Moriscos. The 68th Light Infantry were withdrawn from here by Wellington after some sharp fighting on 20 June.

**On the night of 21 July 1812 a
tremendous storm blew up with
crashes of lightning, thunder and
torrential rain. The camp of the
5th Dragoon Guards was a scene
of pandemonium and chaos as
frightened horses bolted or rode
over their riders sleeping on the
ground. The regiment suffered
18 men hurt, while 31 horses
bolted into the night. The
occurrence of a storm before a
battle was to become an omen of
victory for Wellington's men.
Indeed, similar storms occurred
on the nights preceding Sorauren
and, of course, Waterloo.**

and Light Divisions. The small Allied force suffered 50 casualties in driving the French from the knoll, but there was no French retaliation. The French piquets simply retired 200 yards down to Moriscos itself. That night, Marmont withdrew his army to Aldea Rubia, some six miles to the east.

'DAMNED TEMPTING...'

The situation on 20-22 June was an intriguing one, with both armies passing up the opportunity to attack each other. On 21 June Wellington's force at San Cristobal numbered some 37,000 Anglo-Portuguese infantry, as well as 3,500 cavalry. He could also call upon the 3,000-strong Spanish division of Carlos de España. Marmont, on the other hand, could muster just 28,000 infantry and 2,000 cavalry. Moreover, Wellington possessed a fine position overlooking his French adversary, who himself maintained a dangerous position with little defensive cover. In such a vulnerable position Marmont could not have got away without putting up a fight and

WRJ. 97

Castrejon, the scene of the skirmish on 18 July during which Wellington and Beresford both had to draw their swords to fend off hovering French cavalry which had charged over the hills to the right of this photo.

the odds were firmly in favour of a crushing Allied victory; the Allied cavalry, in spite of its patchy reputation, would surely have had a field day. As he watched and waited for Marmont to attack, Wellington himself is reputed to have said, 'Damned tempting! I have a great mind to attack 'em'. He did not, however, something he may have regretted during the afternoon when the divisions of both Thomières and Foy, numbering just over 9,500 men, arrived to join Marmont's army.

Ironically, while Wellington waited for Marmont to attack, the French marshal was holding a 'council-of-war' with his generals, two of whom, Maucune and Ferey, actually advocated an attack. However, both Clausel and Foy urged Marmont to be more cautious. Foy himself had good reason to remember Vimeiro and Busaco, and did not wish to receive similar treatment. And so Marmont was allowed to march away from what was undoubtedly an extremely dangerous situation. The remarkable thing is that Marmont did not realise this, and appears never to have considered for a moment that Wellington was capable of such an offensive movement. In fact, in his despatch to King Joseph he simply said that he would not attack while his numbers were not at least equal to the Allies and that he withdrew in order to await the arrival of 8,000 reinforcements from Gen. Caffarelli and the Army of the North.

During the next four days Marmont's army manoeuvred to the east of Salamanca with a view to relieving the Salamanca forts. At one stage Marmont even sent some 12,000 men across the Tormes via the fords at Huerta in an attempt to force Wellington into dividing his force. This move was thwarted by a similar move across the Tormes, closer to Salamanca, by Graham with the 1st and 7th Divisions.

At dawn on 27 June the governor of the San Vincente fort signalled that he was capable of prolonging the defence for a further three days. This message increased Marmont's determination to relieve the forts and accordingly he planned a move south. His 40,000-strong army would cross the Tormes at Alba de Tormes from where it would march north-west to Salamanca. Such a move was extremely risky because Wellington, already outnumbering Marmont by nearly 4,000 men, would have the use of Clinton's 6th Division which would have been freed from the siege of the forts, something Marmont would not have known until too late had he executed the move. Ironically, such a march would have brought him to the very same ground as that upon which he was destined to be defeated on 22 July. Before he got underway, however, Marmont received news that the Salamanca forts had surrendered, the march across the Tormes was abandoned and a potentially calamitous move was averted, albeit for a matter of weeks.

The fall of the Salamanca forts was the second of two blows for Marmont in the space of two days. The previous day he had received news from Caffarelli that due to a threat to Bilbao from Sir Home Popham, who was co-operating with Spanish regulars and guerrillas, he would not now be marching to his assistance and would instead march north to avert this new threat. This, along with the fall of the Salamanca forts on 27 June, settled the business as far as Marmont was concerned. He had manoeuvred around Salamanca for the past week or so, often in dangerous situations, in order to attempt the relief of the forts. But now the forts had surrendered and with little immediate prospect of reinforcements, there was little benefit to be gained from remaining any longer.

Therefore, at dawn on 28 June Marmont's army began its withdrawal north-east towards Valladolid and a new defensive position behind the Douro River. Marmont realised such a move would isolate him from Madrid, but it would, on the other hand, take him closer to Bonnet, whose 8th Division was expected from the Asturias. Once Bonnet had joined him Marmont would be able to field an army equal, at least in number, to Wellington's.

There was little movement by either army during the first two weeks of July. The French concentrated behind the Douro between Toro and Tordesillas, while Wellington's massed south of the Douro between La Seca and Rueda. During this period of inactivity the men of both armies bathed regularly in the Douro close to Pollo and it was not uncommon to see both French and British troops in the water at the same time.

On 7 July Marmont was finally joined by Bonnet's division, although unknown to him Caffarelli, Suchet and Soult had each sent despatches to Joseph informing him that they could not spare any men for the Army of Portugal. Joseph was aware of the danger in which this might place him should Marmont be defeated by Wellington. Having weighed up the situation, Joseph recalled all garrisons from Castile in order to reinforce Marmont. However, this valuable 13,000-strong reinforcement, under Joseph himself, did not leave Madrid until 21 July, and did not arrive in time to have any bearing on the outcome of the battle of Salamanca.

The final stage of the preliminaries leading to the battle began on 16 July with a move by Marmont across the Douro. He pushed Bonnet's and Foy's divisions across the river at Toro, while the bulk of his army concentrated at Tordesillas. Then, after Wellington had shifted part of his force to Fuente la Pena and Canizal in anticipation of a French advance south from Toro, the two French divisions swiftly recrossed the Douro, broke down the bridge at Toro and rejoined Marmont's main army

which then crossed the Douro at Tordesillas during the night of 16 July. This move was calculated to wrong-foot Wellington, which in fact it did. Early on the morning of 17 July Marmont's troops poured over the Douro at Tordesillas, passing through the area recently occupied by Wellington's troops who had marched south-west. Fortunately, the Allied commander-in-chief was not totally fooled and, ever suspicious and cautious, he had halted the 4th and Light Divisions, as well as Anson's brigade of cavalry, at Castrejon. The rest of his army, meanwhile, was positioned between Castrillo and Canizal. Once aware of Marmont's real intentions, Wellington decided to pull his rearguard back to rejoin the main body of the army.

Never one to delegate too often, Wellington rode forward himself to initiate the move at daylight on 18 July. As he arrived at Castrejon he

Throughout the long, hot day of 20 July 1812, both armies marched parallel to each other, separated by just a few hundred yards. The situation occurred when Marmont attempted to get around Wellington's left flank as he marched south but each time the French moved further to the east, Wellington did likewise, his men keeping a wary eye on their adversaries over their left shoulders. The two armies parted company at Cantalpino when Wellington moved west towards San Cristobal, Marmont continuing on to the fords over the Tormes at Huerta. Although it appears that Marmont was threatening Wellington's right, it must be remembered that the Allied army was marching south and therefore it was Wellington's left that was threatened.

found Allied cavalry patrols, under Cotton, already engaged with French cavalry who were advancing in strength. There followed a sharp skirmish between Allied cavalry and artillery and French cavalry, supported by a strong column of infantry. Wellington rode forward with Marshal Beresford and their staffs at the precise moment when a squadron of French cavalry charged upon the flank of the Allied guns, sweeping aside a squadron of 12th Light Dragoons behind them. The 12th were thrown back upon their own supporting troops, a squadron of the 11th Light Dragoons. Apparently, in the confusion, a staff officer shouted the wrong order and the 11th turned about, sweeping down on Wellington, Beresford and their staffs, forcing them to draw their swords as the French got in among them. It was a close call, and there was a very real chance that Wellington might have been either killed or captured. In the event, the 11th Light Dragoons, realising the mistake, turned and inflicted heavy losses on the French who were driven off.

PARALLEL MARCHING

Marmont's thrust south initiated a period of complex manoeuvres during which the French marshal attempted to get round Wellington's left flank. However, each French move to the south-east was countered by a similar move by Wellington. On 19 July, in fact, both armies stood motionless in front of each other, separated only by the Guarena River, just to the north of the villages of El Olmo and Vallesa. While Marmont reconnoitred Wellington's position, both sides took the opportunity for some well-earned rest. The men had suffered an exhausting march beneath the searing July sun and any short stop was welcome. As the afternoon wore on neither side moved until, at around 4pm, Marmont's columns lurched back into life and continued marching south-east on

It was across this barren-looking plain that the famous 'parallel march' of both Wellington's and Marmont's armies took place on 20 July. The armies went from right to left of this picture. This photograph was taken from the heights north of Cantalpino.

the right bank of the Guarena. Wellington duly marched in the same direction, on the left bank of the river.

Both armies continued to march on opposite sides of the Guarena River the next day, until Wellington's army reached the Poreda, a tributary of the Guarena. His men continued marching south-east, on the left bank of the Poreda, with Marmont's men keeping to the right bank of the Guarena. This left a triangular area between the two rivers upon which neither army ventured, other than a few cavalrymen. This was the famous parallel march of 20 July, with Wellington's army in three parallel columns, Marmont's in two, each army watching and waiting for any signs of disorder among the other. The two armies got even closer when Marmont ordered his men to cross to the left bank of the Guarena to march south-west in the direction of Cantalpino. It was one of the most memorable days of the Peninsular War, as the two great armies marched at speed, with parade ground precision, within a few hundred yards of each other. Thousands of tramping feet, and hundreds of wheels of the guns and wagons, kicked up huge clouds of dust which added to the stifling heat, and made for an uncomfortable if unforgettable march. Indeed, Marmont himself later said that he had never seen such a magnificent spectacle as the parallel march of two armies of over 40,000 men each at such close quarters.

By midday the two armies neared the village of Cantalpino and unless either of them changed direction they would collide with each other there. Marmont's route just to the north of Cantalpino took him across some higher ground than the Allies and just as Wellington's leading brigades passed through it, the French marshal ordered some of his guns to open fire. Wellington, however, gave orders to his commanders not to return fire, but instead his divisions veered south-west, away from the village, and in doing so refused to give battle.

By late afternoon the two armies had lost sight of each other and Wellington ended the day with his troops occupying the heights of Cabeza Vellosa and Aldea Rubia, a good defensible site. Marmont, meanwhile, occupied a position with his left flank resting upon the fords across the Tormes at Huerta.

The final run up to the battle of Salamanca got underway at dawn on 21 July when Marmont's troops forded the Tormes at Huerta and began filing south. This move left Wellington with little option but to abandon Salamanca, for if he did not he risked having his communications with Ciudad Rodrigo cut. Therefore, on the afternoon of 21 July, the Allied army began to plunge into the Tormes at the fords of Cabrerizos and Santa Marta. This move lasted well into the afternoon, but by nightfall both armies occupied positions running north–south, the right of Marmont's army resting upon Machachon with the left upon Calvarrasa de Arriba. Wellington's army had its left flank upon the Tormes at Santa Marta and its right upon the high ground to the north of the Lesser Arapil hill. The only troops still on the northern bank of the Tormes were D'Urban's Portuguese cavalry and the 3rd Division, under Edward Pakenham.

The night before the battle of Salamanca was marked by a tremendous storm when bolts of lightning caused chaos among the cavalry of both sides. Scores of troopers were injured by their horses who trampled on them in their panic. The rain fell in torrents, and all those present agreed that a more violent storm had seldom been witnessed. For Wellington's men, however, such a storm would soon be seen as an omen of victory, one that would be repeated before Sorauren and, of course, on the eve of Waterloo.

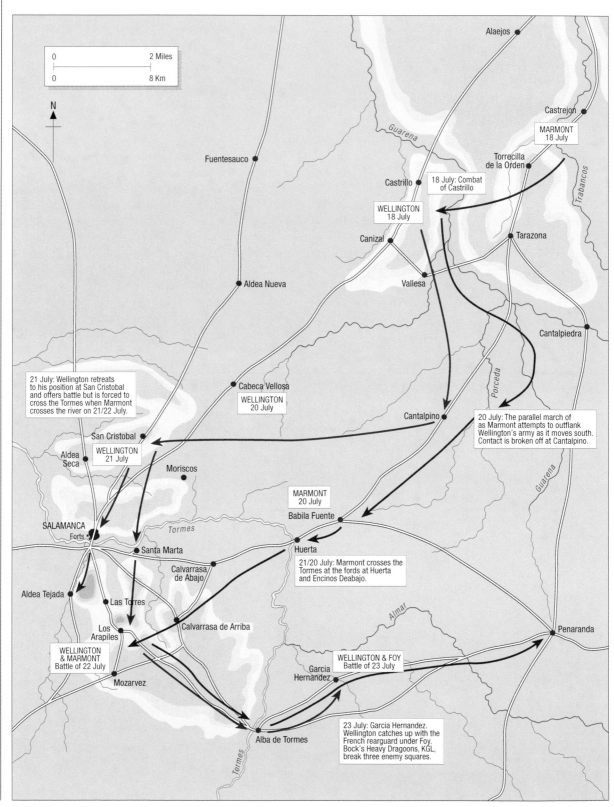

0   2 Miles

0   8 Km

N

Alaejos

Castrejon

Guarena

MARMONT
18 July

Torrecilla
de la Orden

Trabancos

Fuentesauco

Castrillo

18 July: Combat
of Castrillo

WELLINGTON
18 July

Tarazona

Canizal

Vallesa

Aldea Nueva

Cantalpiedra

Porceda

21 July: Wellington retreats
to his position at San Cristobal
and offers battle but is forced to
cross the Tormes when Marmont
crosses the river on 21/22 July.

Cabeca Vellosa

WELLINGTON
20 July

Cantalpino

20 July: The parallel march of
as Marmont attempts to outflank
Wellington's army as it moves south.
Contact is broken off at Cantalpino.

San Cristobal

WELLINGTON
21 July

Aldea
Seca

Moriscos

Guarena

MARMONT
20 July

SALAMANCA
Forts

Tormes

Babila Fuente

Santa Marta

Huerta

Calvarrasa
de Abajo

21/20 July: Marmont crosses the
Tormes at the fords at Huerta
and Encinos Deabajo.

Aldea Tejada

Las Torres

Almar

Penaranda

Los
Arapiles

Calvarrasa de Arriba

WELLINGTON & FOY
Battle of 23 July

WELLINGTON
& MARMONT
Battle of 22 July

Garcia
Hernandez

Mozarvez

23 July: Garcia Hernandez.
Wellington catches up with the
French rearguard under Foy.
Bock's Heavy Dragoons, KGL,
break three enemy squares.

Alba de Tormes

Tormes

THE OPPOSING COMMANDERS

THE BRITISH

The British Army in the Peninsula was commanded by Sir Arthur Wellesley who, following his victory at Talavera in July 1809, had been created Marquis of Wellington. Wellington commanded the army in the Peninsula from the very outset of the campaign in the summer of 1808, until the end of the war in April 1814, without a single spell of home leave, save for a short spell when he was recalled to Britain following the Convention of Cintra. Born in 1769, Wellington had served in Flanders in 1794-95 and, more notably, in India between 1797 and 1804 where he achieved some fine victories, such as Assaye in 1803, which he later described as one of his greatest successes. In 1808 he had been given command of a force destined to embark upon a campaign in Venezuela, following on from Beresford's and Whitelocke's forays in

ABOVE **Sir Arthur Wellesley, 1st Duke of Wellington, 1769-1852. After a painting by Heaphy, depicting him at the siege of San Sebastian. Wellington commanded the Anglo-Portuguese army in the Peninsula between 1808 and 1814 and, save for a period of six months following the Convention of Cintra in August 1808, did so without a single day's leave.**

ABOVE, RIGHT **General Clausel, 1769-1830. Clausel commanded the French army at Salamanca after both Marmont and Bonnet had been incapacitated. His counter-attack after Cole's failure almost won for the French a drawn battle at Salamanca, if not victory itself.**

BELOW, RIGHT **General Maximilien Foy, 1775-1825. Foy commanded the 1st Division of the Army of Portugal at Salamanca, he later wrote his own account of the war in Spain as well as his own memoirs.**

FAR, RIGHT **Sir Galbraith Lowry Cole, 1772-1842. Cole commanded Wellington's 4th Division at Salamanca and was wounded during the battle. He later married on the eve of Waterloo and so missed the great battle there in 1815.**

ABOVE **Sir Dennis Pack, 1772-1823. Pack had been taken prisoner twice during the ill-fated South American campaigns of 1806 and 1807. He served with distinction in the Peninsula and at Waterloo. He commanded a Portuguese brigade at Salamanca.**

ABOVE **Sir James Leith, 1763-1816. Commanded the 5th Division at Salamanca and it was his attack which broke the centre of the French army.**

RIGHT **William Carr Beresford, 1764-1854. Beresford was one of Wellington's most trusted subordinates who nevertheless blotted his copybook by his handling of the army at Albuera on 16 May 1811. He is chiefly remembered for his reorganisation of the Portuguese army in the Peninsula.**

South America in 1806 and 1807. However, at the outbreak of the Peninsular War the force was ordered to Portugal instead. Many of Wellington's problems throughout the early stages of the war until 1812 have been dealt with in the previous chapters. He was greatly assisted by his brother Richard Wellesley, who was British ambassador in Madrid and who proved to be a great help in getting the otherwise dilatory Spaniards to move in support of their British allies.

Wellington had lost the commander of his Light Division, Robert Craufurd, during the assault of Ciudad Rodrigo, as well as a host of fine regimental officers at the bloody storming of Badajoz in April 1812. In spite of these losses, however, he possessed many fine divisional and regimental officers, who would go on to distinguish themselves at Salamanca. His brother-in-law, Edward Pakenham, was to become one such hero. Born in 1778, Pakenham had been with the Peninsular army since 1810 and commanded the 'Fighting' 3rd Division of the army in the absence of the fiery Welshman, Thomas Picton, who had been wounded at Badajoz.

In command of Wellington's 4th Division was Sir Lowry Cole He was an experienced general who had seen service in the Peninsula since 1809. Cole had also been present at the battle of Maida in 1806 and thus had witnessed one of the earliest triumphs of the two-deep British line, a tactic which was to sweep Napoleon's legions aside on several occasions. The 5th Division of the army was commanded by the 49-year old Scot, Sir James Leith, who had distinguished himself at the storming of Badajoz when his division successfully escaladed the San Vincente bastion.

One final word on Wellington's commanders should be reserved for Gen. John Gaspard Le Marchant, the commander of the Heavy Brigade of Cavalry. Since the departure from the Peninsula in 1809 of Henry, Lord Paget – he had run off with Wellington's sister-in-law – Wellington had been without a capable cavalry commander. The Allied cavalry gained a reputation for, as Wellington put it, 'galloping at everything', and had thus become something of a liability within his army. This uncontrollable urge to charge everything in their front on every occasion was demonstrated right up to the final battle of the Napoleonic Wars, Waterloo, on that occasion by the Union Brigade. Le Marchant, however, was a fine cavalry commander and has often been called 'a scientific soldier' on account of his training and knowledge of cavalry. His part in the battle of Salamanca was devastating although, ironically, tragic.

RIGHT **Marshal Andre Massena, duc d'Essling, 1758-1817.** Wellington's most dogged opponent in the Peninsula who served there between 1810 and 1811 before being recalled to Paris in May of that year.

LEFT **General John Gaspard Le Marchant, 1766-1812.** Le Marchant commanded the Heavy Cavalry brigade at Salamanca which demolished eight French battalions during its devastating charge. He was, however, tragically killed towards the end of the charge. One of the most influential soldiers of his age, Le Marchant designed the superb 1796-pattern light cavalry sabre and formed an accompanying system of sword drill.

FAR LEFT **Edward Pakenham 1769-1815.** Pakenham commanded Wellington's 3rd Division in the absence of Thomas Picton who had been wounded at Badajoz. Pakenham was killed in action three years later at New Orleans.

ABOVE **Marshal Auguste Marmont, Duc de Raguse, 1774-1852.** Having superseded Massena the previous year, Marmont commanded the Army of Portugal at Salamanca but was badly wounded early in the action.

THE FRENCH

The French army at Salamanca, the Army of Portugal, was commanded by the 38-year-old Marshal Auguste Marmont, Duc de Raguse. Marmont, a veteran fighter of several campaigns and ADC to Napoleon in 1796, had been appointed to command in Spain on 7 May 1811, replacing Marshal Massena. Marmont had spent his 12 months' command marching and manoeuvring upon the Spanish–Portuguese border, but he had yet to fight a major battle in the Peninsula. Salamanca was to be his first and last.

There were also several fine divisional commanders present, including Gen. Maximilien-Sebastien Foy, the 37-year-old veteran of Vimeiro who had been in the Peninsula since 1808, and who later wrote his own account of the war. Gen. Bertrand Clausel was another skilled commander who had seen widespread service and who had come to Portugal in 1809. The 44-year old Jean-Pierre-François Comte Bonnet, later to assume command of the army at Salamanca upon Marmont's wound, had seen action throughout Europe and had lost an eye in 1793 at Hondschoote. Two other French generals who deserve a mention include Jean-Guillaume-Barthèlemy, Baron Thomières, a veteran of several battles in Italy and an officer of the Lègion d'honneur, who had been wounded at Vimeiro; and finally Antoine-François, Baron Brennier, wounded three times during his career, who had shown great skill in leading his garrison from the fortress of Almeida in May 1811 in the face of a British blockade, much to the annoyance of Wellington. Indeed, this incident is said by Wellington to have turned his victory at Fuentes de Oñoro into a defeat. Both of these last named men played significant roles at the battle of Salamanca.

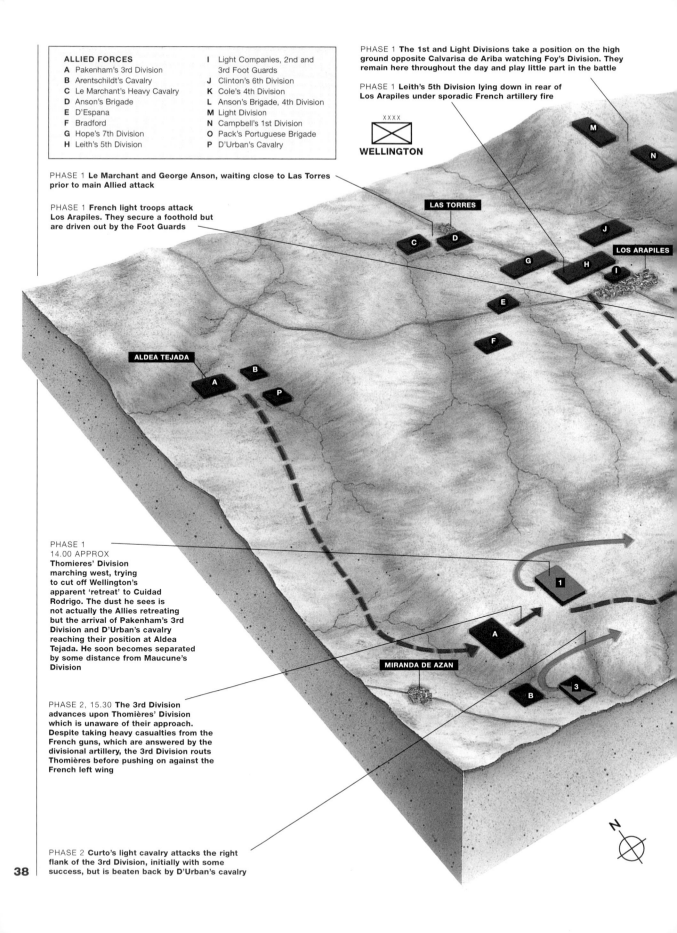

ALLIED FORCES

A Pakenham's 3rd Division
B Arentschildt's Cavalry
C Le Marchant's Heavy Cavalry
D Anson's Brigade
E D'Espana
F Bradford
G Hope's 7th Division
H Leith's 5th Division

I Light Companies, 2nd and 3rd Foot Guards
J Clinton's 6th Division
K Cole's 4th Division
L Anson's Brigade, 4th Division
M Light Division
N Campbell's 1st Division
O Pack's Portuguese Brigade
P D'Urban's Cavalry

PHASE 1 **The 1st and Light Divisions take a position on the high ground opposite Calvarisa de Ariba watching Foy's Division. They remain here throughout the day and play little part in the battle**

PHASE 1 **Leith's 5th Division lying down in rear of Los Arapiles under sporadic French artillery fire**

XXXX
WELLINGTON

PHASE 1 **Le Marchant and George Anson, waiting close to Las Torres prior to main Allied attack**

PHASE 1 **French light troops attack Los Arapiles. They secure a foothold but are driven out by the Foot Guards**

LAS TORRES

LOS ARAPILES

ALDEA TEJADA

PHASE 1
14.00 APPROX
Thomieres' Division marching west, trying to cut off Wellington's apparent 'retreat' to Cuidad Rodrigo. The dust he sees is not actually the Allies retreating but the arrival of Pakenham's 3rd Division and D'Urban's cavalry reaching their position at Aldea Tejada. He soon becomes separated by some distance from Maucune's Division

MIRANDA DE AZAN

PHASE 2, 15.30 **The 3rd Division advances upon Thomières' Division which is unaware of their approach. Despite taking heavy casualties from the French guns, which are answered by the divisional artillery, the 3rd Division routs Thomières before pushing on against the French left wing**

PHASE 2 **Curto's light cavalry attacks the right flank of the 3rd Division, initially with some success, but is beaten back by D'Urban's cavalry**

N

38

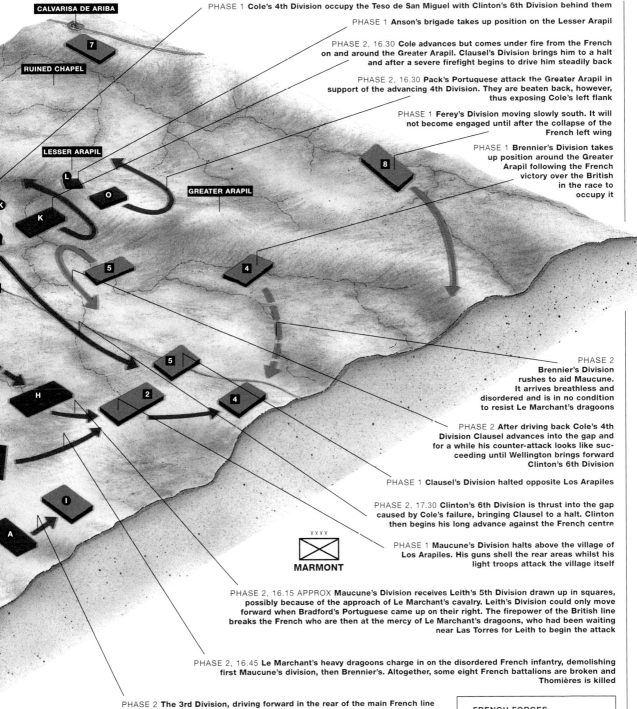

CALVARISA DE ARIBA

RUINED CHAPEL

LESSER ARAPIL

GREATER ARAPIL

PHASE 1 **Cole's 4th Division occupy the Teso de San Miguel with Clinton's 6th Division behind them**

PHASE 1 **Anson's brigade takes up position on the Lesser Arapil**

PHASE 2, 16.30 **Cole advances but comes under fire from the French on and around the Greater Arapil. Clausel's Division brings him to a halt and after a severe firefight begins to drive him steadily back**

PHASE 2, 16.30 **Pack's Portuguese attack the Greater Arapil in support of the advancing 4th Division. They are beaten back, however, thus exposing Cole's left flank**

PHASE 1 **Ferey's Division moving slowly south. It will not become engaged until after the collapse of the French left wing**

PHASE 1 **Brennier's Division takes up position around the Greater Arapil following the French victory over the British in the race to occupy it**

PHASE 2 **Brennier's Division rushes to aid Maucune. It arrives breathless and disordered and is in no condition to resist Le Marchant's dragoons**

PHASE 2 **After driving back Cole's 4th Division Clausel advances into the gap and for a while his counter-attack looks like succeeding until Wellington brings forward Clinton's 6th Division**

PHASE 1 **Clausel's Division halted opposite Los Arapiles**

PHASE 2, 17.30 **Clinton's 6th Division is thrust into the gap caused by Cole's failure, bringing Clausel to a halt. Clinton then begins his long advance against the French centre**

PHASE 1 **Maucune's Division halts above the village of Los Arapiles. His guns shell the rear areas whilst his light troops attack the village itself**

xxxx

MARMONT

PHASE 2, 16.15 APPROX **Maucune's Division receives Leith's 5th Division drawn up in squares, possibly because of the approach of Le Marchant's cavalry. Leith's Division could only move forward when Bradford's Portuguese came up on their right. The firepower of the British line breaks the French who are then at the mercy of Le Marchant's dragoons, who had been waiting near Las Torres for Leith to begin the attack**

PHASE 2, 16.45 **Le Marchant's heavy dragoons charge in on the disordered French infantry, demolishing first Maucune's division, then Brennier's. Altogether, some eight French battalions are broken and Thomières is killed**

PHASE 2 **The 3rd Division, driving forward in the rear of the main French line**

BATTLE OF SALAMANCA

22 July 1812, Dawn – 19.00, viewed from the south-west showing Pakenham's attack on Thomières' Division and the repulse of the attack of Cole's Division and Pack's Portuguese on the Greater Arapile

FRENCH FORCES
1 Thomières' Division
2 Maucune's Division
3 Carto's Light Cavalry
4 Brennier's Division
5 Clausel's Division
6 French skirmishers attacking Los Arapiles
7 Foy's Division
8 Ferey's Division
9 Sarrut's Division (not yet arrived)

THE BATTLE

The morning of 22 July dawned warm and sunny, which came as a welcome relief to the French and Allied troops after their soaking the previous night. The hot sun soon dried out the ground enough for clouds of dust to be kicked up by the two armies as they marched into position.

The Allied position extended from the River Tormes at Santa Marta on their left, along a range of heights running south to the Lesser Arapil. D'Urban's cavalry and the 3rd Division were still on the north bank of the Tormes, watching the ford at Cabrerizos. Marmont occupied the ridge facing the Allies, stretching from the Tormes on the French right flank, to Calvarisa de Arriba on their left. Just in front of them lay the ruined chapel of Nuestra Senora de la Pena, occupied by some picquets of the British 7th Division, who were camped in some woods on the slopes to the west, with the 1st and Light Divisions in front. A valley or ravine separated the two heights, through which a small stream, the Pelegracia, flowed. During the morning Marmont began to bring the remainder of his army across the river and soon it began to move slowly south, his intention being to turn south-west and cut across the main road to Ciudad Rodrigo, Wellington's line of retreat to Portugal.

The first skirmishing of the day took place at the ruined chapel, when Marmont, unhappy at having a British presence so close to his own position, ordered Foy's voltigeurs to drive the British piquets back across the stream. Wellington countered this by sending forward the whole of the 68th and the 2nd Caçadores who drove the French back. This peculiar, isolated, episode took place a half-a-mile from the main Allied position, but perhaps demonstrates Wellington's determination to screen his main force from the prying eyes of Marmont's forward troops. The fight died down some time after noon, when both the 68th and 2nd Caçadores were withdrawn and replaced by some companies of the 95th Rifles, whom Marmont made no further attempt to drive off. Indeed, during the morning the 7th Division was pulled back from its position to join the 5th and 6th Divisions which were hidden from view close to the village of Carbajosa. Cole's 4th Division, meanwhile, occupied a position on and around the Lesser Arapil.

Having ridden frantically across from the village of Los Arapiles, Wellington joins his brother-in-law, Edward Pakenham, commanding the 3rd Division, and directs him to 'drive everything before him to the devil'. (After a painting by Caton-Woodville)

The 3rd Division smashing into Thomières' division above Miranda de Azan on 22 July 1812, to begin the main action at Salamanca. Thomières was killed in the fight and his entire divisional artillery captured. As usual, anachronisms abound in Caton-Woodville's painting, such as the bearskins worn by the grenadiers.

THE BATTLEFIELD

The battlefield area is dominated by two striking hills, known locally as the *Hermanitos* ('two brothers'), or the Arapiles, as they are better known. The right flank of Wellington's line rested upon the Lesser Arapil, a round hill about 100 feet high. This rugged hill is of easy ascent, and affords a good view of the surrounding area. About 600 yards to the south lies a much longer hill, the Greater Arapil. It is about 300 yards long and a few feet higher than the Lesser Arapil. Its northern face is fairly easy to climb, but the other sides are much steeper. Away to the south of the Greater Arapil lay an extensive wood which was later to provide the French troops with some sanctuary from the pursuing Allied army.

The Lesser Arapil itself is located at the hinge of an L-shaped range of hills which run north from the Lesser Arapil for about one mile, and west for a similar distance. The western hills are fairly low, unlike the northern branch which, towards the northern end, are fairly high in places. This L-shaped ridge lies within another, much larger L-shaped ridge which was to form the French position during the battle. The Greater Arapil formed the hinge of this ridge which ran north for about two miles and west for about three miles, as far as the village of Miranda de Azan. To the west of the two Arapiles hills lies the village of Los Arapiles itself, tucked away at the foot of a gradual slope which leads up to a ridge beyond which lay a wide valley, about 1,200 yards wide. The southern border of this valley was marked by another, slightly higher, ridge, which ran west as far as the village of Miranda. From the village to this ridge was a distance of about one mile. To the north of Los Arapiles lies the village of Las Torres and between the two, and just to the east of the former, is the hill of San Miguel, from which Wellington would observe much of the battle.

Wellington's army initially occupied a position running north–south, facing Marmont's army which was drawn up on the slopes opposite them with their left flank resting upon Calvarisa de Arriba. However, as the

MARMONT'S MANOEUVRES 21-22 JULY 1812

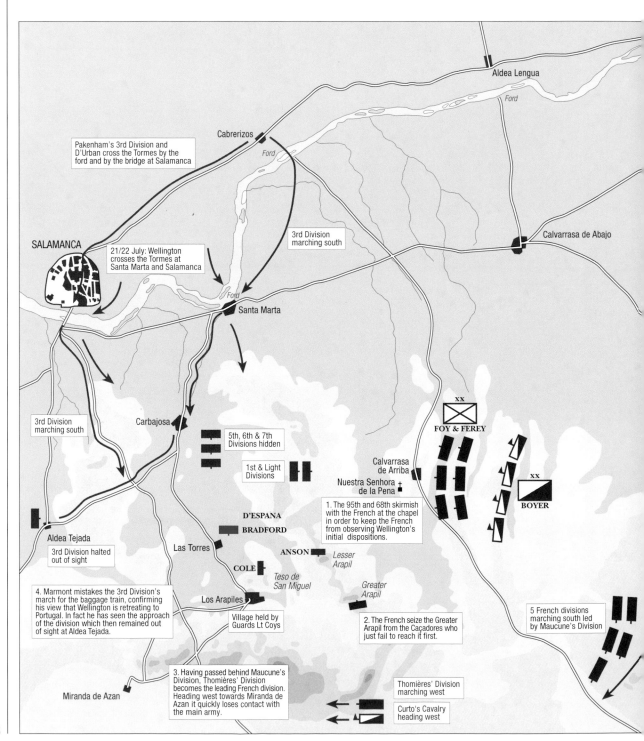

Aldea Lengua

Ford

Cabrerizos

Ford

Pakenham's 3rd Division and D'Urban cross the Tormes by the ford and by the bridge at Salamanca

Calvarrasa de Abajo

3rd Division marching south

SALAMANCA

21/22 July: Wellington crosses the Tormes at Santa Marta and Salamanca

Ford

Santa Marta

XX
FOY & FEREY

3rd Division marching south

Carbajosa

5th, 6th & 7th Divisions hidden

Calvarrasa de Arriba

XX
BOYER

1st & Light Divisions

Nuestra Senhora de la Pena

1. The 95th and 68th skirmish with the French at the chapel in order to keep the French from observing Wellington's initial dispositions.

Aldea Tejada

3rd Division halted out of sight

D'ESPANA

BRADFORD

Las Torres

ANSON

Lesser Arapil

COLE

Teso de San Miguel

Greater Arapil

4. Marmont mistakes the 3rd Division's march for the baggage train, confirming his view that Wellington is retreating to Portugal. In fact he has seen the approach of the division which then remained out of sight at Aldea Tejada.

Los Arapiles

Village held by Guards Lt Coys

2. The French seize the Greater Arapil from the Caçadores who just fail to reach it first.

5 French divisions marching south led by Maucune's Division

3. Having passed behind Maucune's Division, Thomières' Division becomes the leading French division. Heading west towards Miranda de Azan it quickly loses contact with the main army.

Miranda de Azan

Thomières' Division marching west

Curto's Cavalry heading west

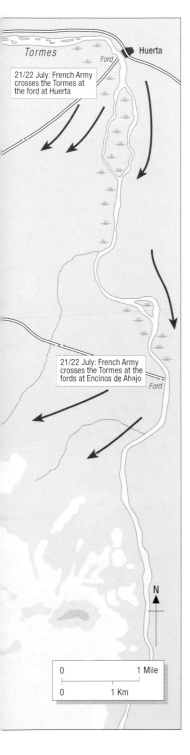

Tormes

Huerta

Ford

21/22 July: French Army crosses the Tormes at the ford at Huerta

21/22 July: French Army crosses the Tormes at the fords at Encinos de Ahajo

Ford

N

| 0 | 1 Mile |
| 0 | 1 Km |

morning wore on it became obvious that the French were moving south, extending their left, and Wellington realised that he needed to occupy the Greater Arapil. His troops already held the Lesser Arapil, but in the half-light of the early morning he had not really appreciated the significance of the Greater Arapil whose bulky mass lay silhouetted further to the south. The occupation of both hills would have given him a position of great strength, providing two strong bastions which would be difficult to assault. Also, should the French attempt to march round his right flank they would have to negotiate the dense wood which lay to the south of the Greater Arapil. In the event, at around 8am, Marmont, seeing that the Greater Arapil was devoid of Allied troops, sent a body of skirmishers to occupy it at once, and there was a race between his men and the 7th Portuguese Caçadores, who Wellington had also sent forward. The French infantry proved to be too quick for the Portuguese, and after a swift but heavy exchange of musketry, the Caçadores were driven back. With the Greater Arapil in his hands Marmont began moving five of his divisions, those of Clausel, Brennier, Maucune, Thomières and Sarrut, to the wood which lay to the south. Here, the French assembled to await further orders, while Foy's division remained at Calvarrasa de Arriba.

As the Greater Arapil was the pivot for Marmont's army, so the Lesser Arapil proved the pivot for Wellington who, upon realising that the French were now in a position to threaten his right flank, altered his position. Leith's 5th Division was brought about to face south on the right of Cole, still close to the Lesser Arapil, with Clinton's 6th Division behind Cole, and Hope's 7th Division in support of Leith, behind the village of Los Arapiles. The 1st and Light Divisions, meanwhile, were still in position running north–south and facing east opposite Calvarisa de Arriba. Indeed, these two divisions were to spend the day kicking their heels in frustration away from the main area of fighting, all, that is, except the light companies of the Foot Guards, which were brought up to defend the village of Los Arapiles. Coupled with this shift in position Wellington had ordered Pakenham's 3rd Division and D'Urban's cavalry to move to Aldea Tejada, just to the west of the Ciudad Rodrigo road, in order to support any Allied retreat or to act as an independent force,

should the occasion for an offensive arise. These troops crossed the Tormes by the bridge at Salamanca and by the fords at Cabrerizos.

About an hour before noon, Marmont climbed to the top of the Greater Arapil and began scanning the Allied position. It is possible, even on a fairly hazy day, to see as far as Salamanca itself, the towers of the two cathedrals dominating the distant skyline. From his position Marmont would have been able to see most of the ground in rear of the Allied position. He would certainly have been able to see the ground between Los Arapiles and Las Torres (see the photograph on page 66). Hence, the 4th, 5th, 6th and 7th Divisions would have been visible, as would the 1st and Light Divisions, still facing east opposite Calvarisa de Arriba. The ground immediately behind the Lesser Arapil would have remained hidden, however.

The 12th Light Dragoons charging at Salamanca, 22 July 1812. The Heavy Cavalry brigade naturally drew most praise for its conduct during the battle but the light dragoons did equally fine work on the day, and throughout the campaign as a whole. They are shown here wearing Tarleton helmets which were replaced later by the bell-topped helmet of which Wellington complained, it being very similar to that already worn by the French. After a painting by Granville Baker.

FRENCH MANOEUVRES

Marmont was obviously under the impression that Wellington was in retreat towards Ciudad Rodrigo. Indeed, the Allied baggage train had already been reported moving off along the road, and his supposition appeared to be confirmed when clouds of dust were seen in the distance leaving Salamanca at speed in the same direction.

Marmont's first conclusion was that Wellington was mustering his troops for an attack on Bonnet's division, which occupied the ground around the Greater Arapil, and was somewhat isolated from the other French divisions. In fact, Wellington himself had considered such a move and apparently ordered the 1st Division to be brought to a state of readiness. However, Beresford persuaded him to abandon the idea. Unfortunately for Marmont, this was to be only a temporary reprieve as the blow, when it did come a few hours later, was to prove even more decisive.

The day wore on and still there was no action, other than the occasional crackle of musketry from the heights around Nuestra Senhora de la Pena, as the British and French piquets sniped at each other. Marmont, meanwhile, continued to gaze out from the Greater Arapil and saw clouds of dust rising in the west, the ground having been thoroughly dried out by the hot sun. There was no doubt in his mind: Wellington was retreating. At about 2pm, therefore, his army lumbered into motion and began moving slowly westwards across the low heights in front of it. This range of heights stretched for about three miles as far as the village of Miranda de Azan. Stretching away beneath them was an undulating plain, about a mile wide, at the foot of which lay the village of Los Arapiles. Marmont's intention was to sever the road to Ciudad Rodrigo and fight Wellington with his army penned in against the Tormes with Salamanca at his back. It seemed quite simple.

The clouds of dust thrown up by Wellington's men did not mark the trail of a retreating army, however, for they were caused by the tramping feet of some 3,600 men of Pakenham's 3rd Division, as well as D'Urban's 482 cavalry. By 2pm Pakenham had reached his position at Aldea Tejada,

ABOVE RIGHT **Wellington and some of his staff at the battle of Salamanca, 22 July 1812.**

British and French infantry clash at Salamanca. The British troops are shown incorrectly wearing the 1812 Belgic shako, which was rarely worn, if at all, in the Peninsula. The town itself can be seen in the background, much closer to the battlefield than it actually is. After a painting by Simkin.

The 'Jingling Johnny', captured from the French 101st Regiment by the 88th (Connaught Rangers) at Salamanca.

just to the west of the Ciudad Rodrigo road and halted in a fold in the ground, hidden from view from all but those Allied officers on the highest point of Wellington's main position. Wellington's army was now arrayed in battle order, forming an L-shape, with the 1st and Light Divisions facing east, and the 4th, 5th, 6th and 7th Divisions facing south, with Pakenham's 3rd Division hidden away at Aldea Tejada.

Marmont's divisions, meanwhile, were on the move, noisily engaged in what they assumed was a resumption of the race which had been run throughout the last few days of manoeuvring north of Salamanca. The leading French division, Maucune's, halted at a point opposite Los Arapiles. Skirmishers went forward to the southern edge of the village, while Maucune's guns opened fire on the village itself and the slopes behind. This artillery fire was returned by the guns of Sympher's battery of the 4th Division and by two guns atop the Lesser Arapil. These latter guns were quickly silenced, however, by French artillery which had been manhandled to the top of the Greater Arapil. Maucune had marched west with the divisions of Thomières and Clausel in support. However, Thomières, instead of merely halting his division behind Maucune, passed to the rear of him and continued marching towards Miranda de Azan. In fact, Marmont's left wing was disappearing away to the west without any support from the French centre or right.

The potentially disastrous manoeuvre was not lost on Wellington when he was told of it. The story of Wellington's 'Salamanca lunch' is almost as well known as the outcome of the battle. While the Allied commander-in-chief was 'stumping about and munching' on a piece of cold chicken, an aide-de-camp suddenly came racing into the courtyard of the farm, and told him that the French were extending to their left. The accounts of just what happened next vary. Wellington is often reported as throwing the leg of chicken over his shoulder before leaping on his horse to take a look for himself. He is also quoted as exclaiming either 'By God! That will do!', or 'The devil they are! Give me the glass quickly'. Whatever the truth, there can be little doubting his rush of excitement when he saw Thomières' error. A brief look through his telescope was enough and, snapping it shut, he turned to Gen. Alava, his Spanish

Royal Horse Artillery teams coming into action in the Peninsula. The RHA troops of Ross, Macdonald and Bull were present at Salamanca. It was a shell fired from one of Dyneley's guns on top of the Lesser Arapil which severely wounded Marmont.

liaison officer, and said calmly, 'Mon cher Alava, Marmont est perdu.'

So, what exactly had Wellington seen? Well, from his position on the Teson de San Miguel, just to the east of the village of Los Arapiles, he could see quite clearly Maucune's division as it halted on the heights immediately to the south of the village. Behind Maucune, Thomières' division was continuing its march west towards Miranda de Azan, while Clausel's division, sent to support Maucune, had stopped after debouching from the woods to the south of the Greater Arapil. The main error was being committed by Thomières who, instead of halting in support of Maucune, continued his march west, imagining a resumption of the 'race' of the previous few days. Before too long a considerable gap had opened between his division and that of Maucune. With the French columns strung out along the heights in front of him, Wellington knew that his moment had come – and he was quick to seize it.

Wellington was soon in full flight, riding towards Aldea Tejada, where Pakenham's 3rd Division and D'Urban's cavalry had arrived unseen at about 2pm. Such was the speed of Wellington's ride – he was an accomplished horseman – that it is said he rode alone for the greater part of the three miles, with his staff trying desperately to keep up with him. It was 3.45pm and it must have been a very dramatic scene as the lone horseman came galloping across the dry, dusty ground with the eyes of every man of

British heavy dragoons in action at Salamanca. Note their old cocked hats, still worn at the time, prior to their replacement by the crested helmet. A negro trumpeter in a white uniform can be seen at left.

the 3rd Division strained anxiously upon him. Wellington found the 3rd Division waiting patiently in their ranks with Pakenham at their head. The commander-in-chief rode up to Pakenham, his brother-in-law, and said simply, 'Edward, move on with the 3rd Division, take those heights in your front, and drive everything before you.' 'I will, my Lord,' replied Pakenham, at which the two men shook hands before parting. Having given the 3rd Division its orders, Wellington turned about and a few minutes later was doing the same to Leith's 5th Division. This is a prime example of Wellington's method of command, and his unwillingness to delegate responsibility to others. Perhaps on this occasion, he recognised the importance of the task given to Pakenham and was not prepared to risk his orders being incorrectly delivered by an aide.

THE ADVANCE OF THE 3RD DIVISION

While Pakenham's division moved off towards Miranda de Azan, Wellington was riding back towards the Allied divisions mustered behind the Teson de San Miguel. En route, orders were despatched to Arentschildt, who was ordered to join D'Urban covering Pakenham's division, and to Bradford, Espana and Cotton, all of whom were soon on the move in support of Leith. Leith, in fact, was the first to receive his orders when Wellington arrived at the Teson de San Miguel. Upon the

arrival of Bradford's Portuguese brigade on his right, Leith's 5th Division was to advance over the Teson and attack Maucune's division which was still on the heights above Los Arapiles. All being well, when Leith attacked he should be able to see Pakenham further to the west as the 3rd Division struck home against Thomières. On Leith's left, meanwhile, Cole was ordered to attack with the 4th Division.

A short time afterwards, the light companies of both the 4th and 5th Divisions, as well as Pack's Portuguese brigade, were stretching out into the Arapiles Valley and were soon making their way towards the crest of the ridge opposite to open fire against their French counterparts. Meanwhile, the main bodies of these units scrambled to their feet to await the order to advance. This, of course, exposed them to the fire of the French artillery, the British and Portuguese having spent the afternoon lying down. This punishment continued for some 40 minutes or so as Leith, Cole and Pack waited for Bradford to come up. Finally, Bradford's Portuguese arrived and the moment had come for Wellington's masterstroke.

It will be easier to follow the battle of Salamanca by beginning with the first action of the afternoon, at Miranda de Azan, and with Pakenham's devastating attack on Thomières' division. However, between 3pm and 4pm the French army lost its commander-in-chief. As Marmont gazed out to the west to watch the progress of his divisions he suddenly realised, to his horror, that not only was Maucune far too close to the village of Los Arapiles, but that Thomières' division, which should have been in support, was pressing too far to the west. Marmont quickly saw the dangerous gap which had appeared between the two divisions and knew that Wellington had only to cross the Arapiles valley and the day would be as good as his. It is somewhat ironic that for once, Marmont appeared to take a leaf out of Wellington's book and decided to come down from the Greater Arapil in order to ride away and take charge of his left wing himself, rather than simply send an order to Thomières to halt via an aide. However, whereas Wellington was able to

British cavalry in action at Salamanca, while a French officer protects an Imperial Eagle, at right.

Officer and riflemen of the 95th Rifles. Probably the most famous British regiment of the Peninsular War, it nevertheless played very little part in the victory at Salamanca.

give his crucial order in person to Pakenham, Marmont was injured as he scrambled down the steep side of the hill by a British shell and left with a serious wound to his arm and ribs. Indeed, the rumour, false as it turned out, went round the British ranks after the battle that he had been killed. With Marmont carried from the field, command passed to Bonnet but, with a singular stroke of bad luck, he too was wounded afterwards, and by 6pm the French army had its third commander of the day, Clausel.

Upon receipt of Wellington's order to advance, Pakenham had formed his division into four columns, the outer two consisting of D'Urban's cavalry, the third made up of Wallace's and Power's brigades, and the fourth column of Campbell's brigade. The division marched in column of lines, a formation which, when the time came, would allow it to form into line without halting. Pakenham's advance, of some two and a half miles, was hidden from the enemy's view by a low range of wooded

THE ATTACK BY LEITH'S 5TH DIVISION
At about 16.40 Leith's 5th Division, after enduring a prolonged period under fire from French artillery, began its attack on Maucune's division above the village of Los Arapiles. The 5th Division advanced with Greville's brigade in front, the 3/1st, 1/9th, the 2/30th and 2/44th, and Spry's Portuguese, the 3rd and 15th Lines. When the 5th

Division reached the crest of the heights they found Maucune's divison drawn up in squares, probably due to the fact that they could see Le Marchant's cavalry advancing on Leith's right flank. In the ensuing contest the British firepower broke the squares and caused the French to break formation, just as Le Marchant's cavalry arrived to complete the rout.

hills to their front. Thomières was completely unaware of the advancing 3rd Division, and had not even taken the precaution of protecting his column with cavalry. Indeed, Curto's light cavalry division which accompanied him appears to have ridden parallel with the centre of the French column, rather than at the head of the column or on its flank. D'Urban himself had ridden on ahead with two ADCs and, peering through some trees, saw that the head of Thomières' division was passing across the right flank of Pakenham's division, which was marching obliquely across Thomières. D'Urban rode back and, gathering his three Portuguese cavalry squadrons about him, with the 11th Portuguese and two squadrons of the 14th Light Dragoons in support, swept from the cover of the trees and charged in among the foremost French company. Two squadrons of the Portuguese dragoons suffered considerably from French fire, but the third squadron, falling upon the unformed left flank of the French column, charged home with some success and broke a

The battle of Salamanca, 22 July 1812. This somewhat stylised engraving shows the battle from the French perspective. Salamanca can just be seen in the distance with the village of Los Arapiles in the centre. Wellington's divisions can be seen in the distance in line.

The small chapel of Nuestra Senhora de la Pena. The chapel lay a mile and a half in front of Wellington's initial position on 22 July. It was occupied by piquets of the 7th Division for a time and was the scene of the early fighting on 22 July involving the 68th, 2nd Cacadores and the 95th Rifles.

whole battalion. The attack had the desired effect of driving the head of the column back upon its succeeding files but, more significantly, it alerted Thomières to the perilous, not to say fatal, situation in which he suddenly found himself.

Thomières' division was strung out along the heights running east from the summit of the Pico de Miranda for a distance of some 2000 yards. His division consisted of three regiments, the 101st, 62nd and the 1st, numbering some eight battalions between them, marching one after the other but with dangerous intervals between them. As if the appearance of D'Urban's cavalry on his flank was not enough to send him into a near panic, Thomières' blood must surely have been chilled by the sudden appearance of Pakenham's 'Fighting' 3rd Division, probably the most fearsome division in the whole of Wellington's fine army. Pakenham's men burst from the trees opposite the Pico de Miranda at a distance of around 500 yards. The oblique advance of Pakenham's men, coupled with their formation in three columns, enabled them to deploy without having to halt. They simply brought up their right shoulders and in a few moments had formed a line from open column, with Wallace's brigade leading.

As soon as Thomières and his men recovered from the shock of having clashed with Allied cavalry, he ordered some 20 guns to be brought forward along the top of the crest towards which the 3rd Division was advancing. These guns began to take their toll on Pakenham's men who advanced into the fire of grape and round shot. At the same time, Curto's light cavalry division finally got into the action, charging in on the right flank of Pakenham's line where the British 1/5th attacked, suffering 126 casualties. Fortunately, Arentschild's

An unusual view of the two Arapiles looking south-west from the initial French position on the morning on 22 July. The Greater Arapil is visible on the skyline to the left, with the Lesser Arapil on the right. Wellington's initial position ran behind the skyline on the right of this photo. Marmont's army would have moved from right to left across the immediate foreground to sweep south to gain the Greater Arapil. They then turned west to form the 'L' shaped line which caused Wellington to shift his position also.

hussars were thrown into the fray, breaking their French adversaries and sending them back upon their own lines. By now British skirmishers were beginning to swarm up the hill to the summit of the Pico de Miranda where they were met half-heartedly by a more numerous French skirmish line whose fire was somewhat ineffective. Thomières' guns, however, took a much heavier toll of the Allied infantry, although this fire was in turn answered by the divisional battery of Douglas's 3rd Division, which began to send shot up the hill against the French right.

The French skirmishers were sent reeling back upon the main body of the French column which struggled to deploy on the crest of the Pico de Miranda, a task made yet more difficult by the ominous and determined advance of Wallace's brigade which grew closer by the minute. They did, however, manage to get off one effective volley which hit scores of Connaught Rangers, but still the 88th came on, their steady, determined advance causing an unsettling effect within the French

Another view of Wellington's initial position as seen from the chapel of Nuestra Senhora de la Pena. Wellington's troops were positioned on the reverse slope of the ridge in the distance. The 1st and Light Divisions remained here during the battle watching Foy's division.

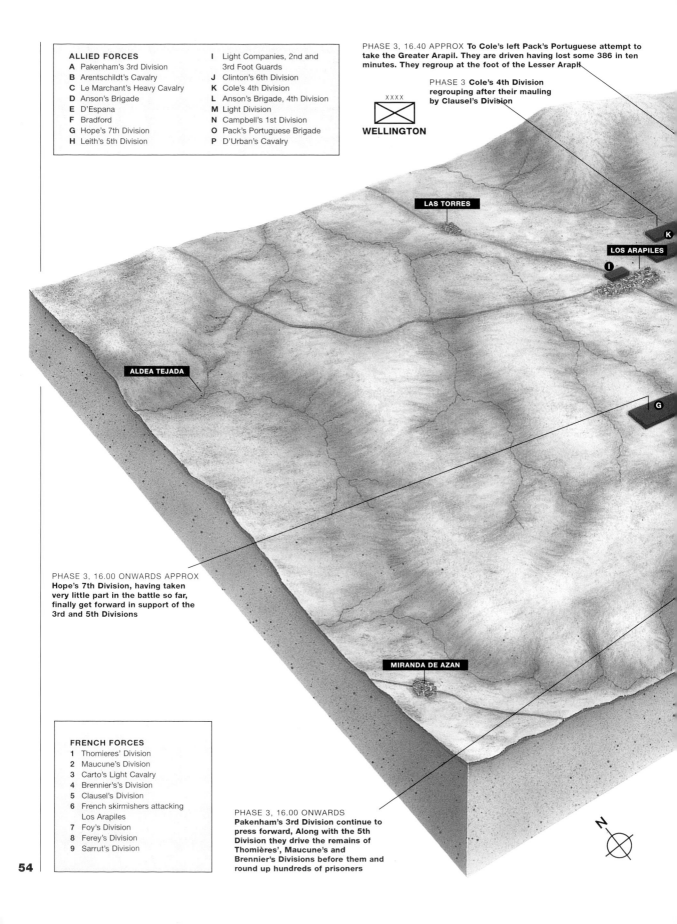

ALLIED FORCES
- **A** Pakenham's 3rd Division
- **B** Arentschildt's Cavalry
- **C** Le Marchant's Heavy Cavalry
- **D** Anson's Brigade
- **E** D'Espana
- **F** Bradford
- **G** Hope's 7th Division
- **H** Leith's 5th Division
- **I** Light Companies, 2nd and 3rd Foot Guards
- **J** Clinton's 6th Division
- **K** Cole's 4th Division
- **L** Anson's Brigade, 4th Division
- **M** Light Division
- **N** Campbell's 1st Division
- **O** Pack's Portuguese Brigade
- **P** D'Urban's Cavalry

PHASE 3, 16.40 APPROX **To Cole's left Pack's Portuguese attempt to take the Greater Arapil. They are driven having lost some 386 in ten minutes. They regroup at the foot of the Lesser Arapil**

PHASE 3 **Cole's 4th Division regrouping after their mauling by Clausel's Division**

XXXX
WELLINGTON

LAS TORRES

LOS ARAPILES

ALDEA TEJADA

PHASE 3, 16.00 ONWARDS APPROX
Hope's 7th Division, having taken very little part in the battle so far, finally get forward in support of the 3rd and 5th Divisions

MIRANDA DE AZAN

FRENCH FORCES
1. Thomieres' Division
2. Maucune's Division
3. Carto's Light Cavalry
4. Brennier's's Division
5. Clausel's Division
6. French skirmishers attacking Los Arapiles
7. Foy's Division
8. Ferey's Division
9. Sarrut's Division

PHASE 3, 16.00 ONWARDS
Pakenham's 3rd Division continue to press forward, Along with the 5th Division they drive the remains of Thomières', Maucune's and Brennier's Divisions before them and round up hundreds of prisoners

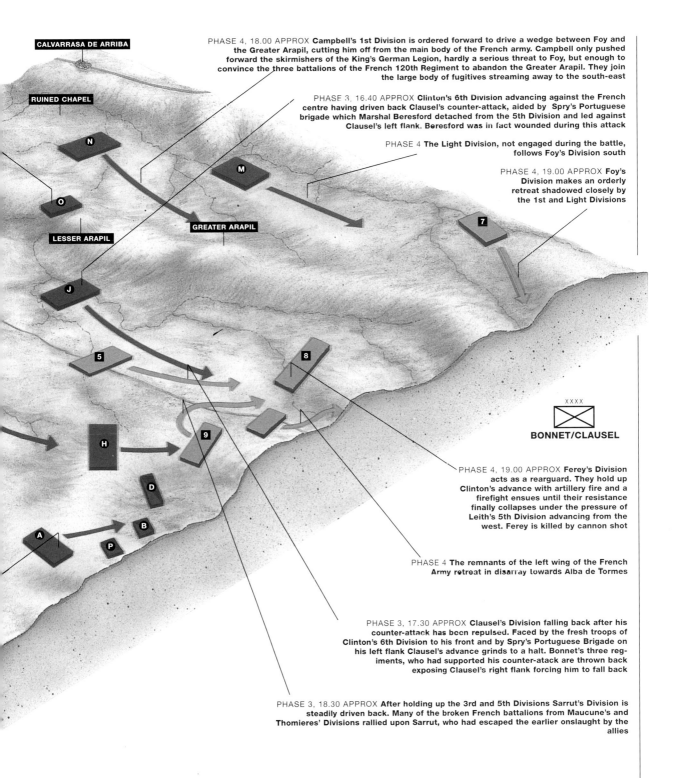

CALVARRASA DE ARRIBA

RUINED CHAPEL

N

O

LESSER ARAPIL

J

GREATER ARAPIL

M

5

H

8

9

D

B

A

P

7

xxxx
⊠
BONNET/CLAUSEL

PHASE 4, 18.00 APPROX Campbell's 1st Division is ordered forward to drive a wedge between Foy and the Greater Arapil, cutting him off from the main body of the French army. Campbell only pushed forward the skirmishers of the King's German Legion, hardly a serious threat to Foy, but enough to convince the three battalions of the French 120th Regiment to abandon the Greater Arapil. They join the large body of fugitives streaming away to the south-east

PHASE 3, 16.40 APPROX Clinton's 6th Division advancing against the French centre having driven back Clausel's counter-attack, aided by Spry's Portuguese brigade which Marshal Beresford detached from the 5th Division and led against Clausel's left flank. Beresford was in fact wounded during this attack

PHASE 4 The Light Division, not engaged during the battle, follows Foy's Division south

PHASE 4, 19.00 APPROX Foy's Division makes an orderly retreat shadowed closely by the 1st and Light Divisions

PHASE 4, 19.00 APPROX Ferey's Division acts as a rearguard. They hold up Clinton's advance with artillery fire and a firefight ensues until their resistance finally collapses under the pressure of Leith's 5th Division advancing from the west. Ferey is killed by cannon shot

PHASE 4 The remnants of the left wing of the French Army retreat in disarray towards Alba de Tormes

PHASE 3, 17.30 APPROX Clausel's Division falling back after his counter-attack has been repulsed. Faced by the fresh troops of Clinton's 6th Division to his front and by Spry's Portuguese Brigade on his left flank Clausel's advance grinds to a halt. Bonnet's three regiments, who had supported his counter-attack are thrown back exposing Clausel's right flank forcing him to fall back

PHASE 3, 18.30 APPROX After holding up the 3rd and 5th Divisions Sarrut's Division is steadily driven back. Many of the broken French battalions from Maucune's and Thomieres' Divisions rallied upon Sarrut, who had escaped the earlier onslaught by the allies

BATTLE OF SALAMANCA

22 July 1812, 16.00 onwards (approx), The French left and centre crumble. Ferey and Sarrut's attempt to slow the Allied advance, but pressure from more than four Allied divisions causes a complete collapse and the Army of Portugal is swept from the field

The long, box-shaped hill on the right is that behind which Pakenham's 3rd Division halted at Aldea Tejada. The village itself lies behind the hill and it was from here, across the foreground, that the 3rd Division advanced. The woods, present in 1812, have completely gone.

ranks. When Major Murphy, commander of the 88th, was shot dead in front of his men there was no holding them. Seeing Murphy's lifeless corpse being dragged along by his horse, the 88th were whipped into a fury and when Pakenham, shouting to make himself heard above the din, gave the order to 'let them loose', they launched a frenzied attack on their French adversaries who paid a terrible price for the death of the 88th's officer.

Indeed, such was the fury of Wallace's attack that Thomières' division crumbled quickly. Thomières himself was killed and his entire divisional battery was captured. The 101st Ligne lost 1,031 out of 1,449 men, while the 62nd Ligne lost 868 out of 1,123. The rear regiment suffered least of all, losing just 231 men out of 1,743. Before long, the shattered remnants of Thomières' division were tumbling back in panic to the east, falling back before Pakenham's cheering brigades upon Maucune's division which itself was about to be demolished.

The Pico de Miranda, as seen from the approach of Pakenham's 3rd Division. This hill represents the limit of Thomieres' march, prior to the attack of the 3rd Division. Pakenham's men attacked up these slopes, probably from right to left, to begin their devastating rout of the French.

The village of Miranda de Azan, as seen from the Pico de Miranda. It was on these barren hills that Thomieres' division was smashed by Pakenham's 3rd Division which swung round to attack from right to left.

At around 4.15pm, some 45 minutes after Pakenham had begun his attack, Leith's 5th Division got to its feet behind the Teson de San Miguel to begin its attack. The order was greeted with relief by the men who must have been relieved that their ordeal at the hands of French artillery would soon be at an end. Indeed, Leith himself had spent much of the afternoon riding up and down among his men encouraging them in the face of the pounding enemy artillery. Even so, they still had to wait for Bradford's Portuguese to come up on their right flank before they could begin any forward movement. Finally, Bradford arrived and the order was given for the advance to begin. The men of the 5th Division began filing through the narrow streets of Los Arapiles, and to the right of the

A view of the two Arapiles hills from the Teso de San Miguel. The Lesser Arapil is visible to the left and the Greater to the right. The Teso de San Miguel was Wellington's viewpoint for much of the battle.

THE 3RD DIVISION'S ATTACK AT MIRANDA DE AZAN

The battle of Salamanca opened at the Pico de Miranda, a hill slightly to the north of the village of Miranda de Azan. Thomières' division had outpaced the main French columns until it had become separated by about a mile from the next division, Maucune's. Pakenham's 3rd Division had marched unseen from Aldea de Tejada in four columns. By bringing up their right shoulders they were suddenly in line before bursting out from the cover of the trees which had hidden their advance. They attacked uphill against the surprised French who barely had time to form. The attack was a devastating success for the 3rd Division who swept over the French, capturing the divisional artillery and killing Thomières himself. Pakenham then led his division east, pushing the remnants of Thomières' division before him.

village, having formed two long lines beforehand. The first line consisted of Greville's brigade, the 3/1st, 1/9th, the 1/38th and 2/38th, as well as the 1/4th from Pringle's brigade. The second line was made up of the rest of Pringle's brigade, the 2/4th, 2/30th and 2/44th, along with the 3rd and 5th Line of Spry's Portuguese brigade. As the long lines of Allied infantry set out towards the French positions on the crest above the village, Wellington himself rode between them before retiring to leave the task to Leith.

The advance of Leith's 5th Division must have been as impressive as it was relentless, the men striding forward in the face of a heavy enemy fire, from both French skirmishers and artillery. Leith's own skirmishers threw themselves forward, and slowly but steadily pushed back those of the enemy who withdrew from the slopes in front of the heights to the crest itself, while the French guns also pulled back. In fact, Maucune

pulled his men back to a position on the reverse slope of the crest, as if aping Wellington's own favoured strategy, and yet the French failed to make the tactic work in the same way. Maucune's columns apparently formed themselves into squares, perhaps because they were aware of Le Marchant's heavy cavalry which must have been visible to mounted French officers. The French infantry squares waited some 50 yards behind the crest, anxious fingers twitching on triggers, while all the time the sound of Leith's relentless advance carried from the other side of the ridge. At last, the Allied infantry came into sight over the ridge and then, at the word of command, the French let loose a single volley followed, a moment later, by a volley from Leith's men. The crash was tremendous. One of the first to come reeling back through the smoke was Greville, commanding the leading brigade; his horse had been shot through the head, and its body fell pinning its rider to the ground. Leith himself was badly wounded, while scores of men on both sides fell amid the storm of musketry. In spite of initial French resistance, the contest was quickly decided by the bayonet-wielding British infantry who, with a wild cheer, lowered their steel and rushed at their adversaries who dissolved into a panic-stricken mass of fleeing men.

ABOVE **A view of the main fighting area at Salamanca, as seen from the top of the Greater Arapil. The village of Los Arapiles can be seen away to the right. Cole's 4th Division attacked from right to left across the immediate foreground, whilst Leith's 5th Division attacked south out of the village itself. The damage wrought by Le Marchant's Heavy Cavalry brigade was roughly where the dark patch on the left horizon is.**

Bradford's Portuguese troops had advanced to the crest on Leith's right and, coming into action against the extreme left flank of Maucune's division, had avoided much of the punishment meted out to the 5th Division during its advance. Bradford, in fact, had met with little opposition and simply joined in the pursuit of Maucune's fleeing infantry. Even further to the Allied right could be seen Pakenham's triumphant 3rd Division which was driving the shattered remnants of Thomières' division before it.

LE MARCHANT'S CAVALRY CHARGE

The 5th Division, meanwhile, pressed on against Maucune whose squares had been devastated by Allied firepower. Ironically, this particular formation, most unsuitable for facing enemy infantry, was what was now required by Maucune more than anything else, because pouring over the crest of the ridge, roaring like a burst of thunder, came every fleeing infantryman's worst nightmare – enemy cavalry. What was worse, these cavalrymen, some 1,000 in all, were the men of Le Marchant's heavy cavalry brigade, the 5th Dragoon Guards, with the 3rd and 4th Dragoons. They were armed with long, straight swords, capable of inflicting terrible wounds upon enemy infantry; nowhere was the power of the 1796-pattern heavy cavalry sword more clearly demonstrated than at Salamanca.

Le Marchant's men had been waiting patiently close to the village of Las Torres where Wellington himself had issued Le Marchant with his orders. He was to 'charge in at all hazards' as soon as Leith's infantry had engaged the French at the crest. The commander of the heavy brigade needed no such explanation of this order, and once Leith's battalions reached the crest of the ridge above Los Arapiles he formed his men into two lines, the 5th Dragoon Guards and the 4th Dragoons in front, with

A French view of the main fighting area at Salamanca. The Greater Arapil is on the right and the Lesser on the left. Thomieres' and Maucune's divisions both passed across the foreground heading west. Both Leith's and Cole's divisions fought here, with Cole's division advancing nearer to the Greater Arapil.

From the elevated position of the camera, this picture gives little idea of the height on the right of this picture. It is, however, the ridge over which Leith's 5th Division attacked to find Maucune drawn up in square formation. Le Marchant's cavalry would have charged over this ridge to find the French waiting obligingly for them in this valley. The 3rd Division, meanwhile, would soon be pushing in along the heights in the distance heading south-east. It was somewhere in this valley that Lieutenant Pearce, of the 44th (East Essex) Regiment, captured the 'eagle' of the French 62nd Regiment.

the 3rd Dragoons in the second line. At 4.45pm the three regiments charged forward, passing Bradford's division on their right, and swept round the right flank of Leith's division, whose men turned and cheered as the dragoons emerged from thick, choking clouds of dust and smoke. As the dragoons rode over the top of the crest they found Maucune's beaten battalions falling back in the face of Leith's onslaught. It was the perfect scenario for Le Marchant and for the much-maligned British cavalry to prove that they were capable of delivering the sort of blow that had eluded them since the days of Sahagun and Benavente.

Le Marchant struck at the brigade on Maucune's left and caught two battalions of the 66th Regiment rolling backwards. The French made a desperate attempt to form themselves into a defensible formation, but before they could do so the heavy dragoons were among them, cutting and hewing all around. The two battalions were all but anni-hilated, hundreds throwing down their arms in sur-render, while the survivors fled to the woods to the south-east. The 15th Line were next to feel the full fury of Le Marchant's men and, like the 66th, were soon in full flight towards the woods. As Maucune's battalions streamed away from the field, Brennier's

division hurried to their assistance. Indeed, his leading regiment, the 22nd Line, formed up and unleashed a withering volley into the ranks of Le Marchant's leading squadron, of the 5th Dragoon Guards, who were leading what was by now a brigade which had become mixed together. In spite of the destructive effect of the volley the dragoons could not be stopped and once again they crashed into the ranks of the French infantry. An almighty struggle ensued as the French defended themselves desperately with their muskets against the awesome British broadsword. Indeed, the French only gave way after some fierce fighting on the part of the dragoons who by now had lost all formation. Sadly, their devastating charge was to end in tragedy. Le

THE CAPTURE OF THE EAGLE OF THE 62ND REGIMENT
As the men of Leith's division rounded up prisoners from Maucune's division following the combined attack by Leith and Le Marchant, Lieutenant Pearce, of the 44th Regiment, saw a French officer attempting to hide the eagle of the 62nd Regiment,

which he had unscrewed from its pole, beneath his greatcoat. Pearce demanded the officer hand it over, whereupon a French soldier levelled his bayonet at him, only to be shot by a man from Pearce's company. Pearce carried the eagle off in triumph and it can be seen on page 64.

Marchant, riding with just half a squadron of the 4th Dragoons, came up against the fugitives on the edge of the wood, one of whom levelled his musket and fired, killing Le Marchant. It was his first major action and Wellington's army was thus deprived of one of the painfully few cavalry officers who knew their business. His brigade had done its job, however, and when the exhausted heavy dragoons gave up the pursuit they could reflect upon the fact that they had destroyed some eight battalions of French infantry. 1,500 French prisoners were taken by the 5th Division, while five guns were captured by the 4th Dragoons. They seized the eagle of the 22nd Line and that of the 62nd Regiment, which was taken by Lt. Pearce of the 44th (East Essex) Regiment, one of Pringle's battalions.

The western half of the battlefield was a mass of confusion, but must have presented a very pleasing sight for the Allied army as thousands of beaten Frenchmen streamed away to the south-east with Leith's triumphant 5th Division pushing ever forward. The 3rd and 5th Divisions swept across the battlefield, driving the remains of Thomières'

The front and back views of the Imperial Eagle of the French 62nd Regiment, captured by Lieutenant Pearce of the 44th (East Essex) Regiment.

Maucune's and Brennier's divisions before them, while D'Urban's and Arentschildt's cavalry charged every now and then against any French infantry that attempted to make a stand.

COUNTERATTACK

In fact, there was some sharp fighting between the two armies' cavalry during this period of the battle. Curto's light cavalry brigades inflicted some damage against isolated parties of Le Marchant's brigade, while the 3rd French Hussars drove back the 1st Hussars of the King's German Legion, who were busy herding in French prisoners, and were only beaten back themselves after a hard fight.

With the left wing of Marmont's army dissolved, Wellington might have thought the battle as good as won. However, in the centre of the battlefield things were not going so well for him. In fact, the French almost staged a remarkable comeback. About 20 minutes after Leith's 5th Division began its advance, Cole's 4th Division moved forward across the valley to attack Clausel's division. The division advanced with Ellis' brigade on the right and Stubbs's on the left, with the 7th Caçadores acting as a thick skirmish line. As with the 5th Division, Cole's men suffered during their march from enemy artillery fire, but soon they were ascending the heights upon which Clausel's men were drawn up. Five French battalions engaged five British and Portuguese battalions and within a few minutes the two sides found themselves locked in a furious firefight which must have rekindled memories of Albuera for the fusiliers of Ellis's brigade. The French were driven back some 200 yards, but Cole's men found themselves dangerously exposed, as their attack lost its impetus and Cole himself was badly wounded. Their somewhat perilous situation was due mainly to the failure of Pack's attack on the Greater Arapil on Cole's left flank.

The rocky ledge at the top of the Greater Arapil. It was here that Pack's Portuguese troops were forced to lay down their muskets in order to climb over the chest-high ledge, at which point the French 120th Regiment stepped forward and drove them back with a devastating volley.

Pack had watched the 4th Division as it purposefully strode forward towards Clausel's division and realised that Cole's left flank would be exposed to an attack from Bonnet's troops who were waiting at the foot of the Greater Arapil. Once Cole had engaged Clausel these troops would, in effect, be in Cole's rear. Therefore, Pack took the decision to move against the Greater Arapil himself with his Portuguese brigade. Wellington, in fact, had previously instructed him to attack if the opportunity arose. That opportunity had now arrived and Pack grasped it - although the outcome was not as he would have wished.

Pack threw out the 4th Caçadores to act as skirmishers, while the Portuguese 1st and 16th Lines followed behind in two columns. Pack had decided to make a direct assault on the northern slopes of the Greater Arapil. The Portuguese made good progress and drove back the French skirmishers opposed to them. Their march continued up the slopes of the Greater Arapil to the flat-topped summit where, just a few feet below it, their advance was halted by a rocky ledge of some five feet or so which had to be negotiated first. The Portuguese infantrymen threw down their muskets and began to climb over the ledge, whereupon the French 120th Regiment, who had been waiting at the top, stepped forward and unleashed a devastating volley into the ranks of the Portuguese who were in no position to make any effective resistance. Pack's men were flung from the top of the Arapil and down the slopes with the jubilant French in hot pursuit. Some 386 Portuguese were lost in just ten minutes in their brave attempt to support the 4th Division. With Pack's brigade having been driven back all the way to the Lesser Arapil, Cole's left flank and rear were threatened by three French regiments. Moreover, the 7th Caçadores, which Cole had detached as a covering force, were swept aside by the numerically superior French who now turned on the 4th Division.

The 4th Division was attacked by Clausel's division from the front, and by three of Bonnet's regiments in the left flank. These latter three regiments consisted of fresh troops who found the 4th Division too

A view of the Lesser Arapil from the northern slopes of the Greater Arapil. The 1st and 16th Portuguese Line marched up the slopes to attack the summit in order to cover the advance of Cole's 4th Division which was moving from right to left from beyond the Lesser Arapil.

exhausted to withstand this new French onslaught. The Portuguese 23rd Line, part of Stubbs's brigade, began the retreat on the left of the line, followed in turn by Ellis's brigade and soon both brigades of the 4th Division were in full flight back into the valley at the foot of the Lesser Arapil.

The repulse of the 4th Division and Pack's brigade left a yawning gap in the centre of Wellington's position, and despite the hammering the French had taken elsewhere on the battlefield, Clausel (now in command following successive wounds to Marmont and Bonnet) was presented with the opportunity to salvage something from the wreckage of the day's fighting, perhaps even a French victory. It was certainly a critical point in the battle. Clausel decided to grasp the opportunity with both hands and go for victory, even though behind him Leith and Pakenham were driving everything before them. Having decided upon this bold course of action Clausel threw his division into the gap, supported by three of Bonnet's regiments and by three regiments of Boyer's dragoons.

The ground to the west of the Greater Arapil was soon covered with the dark, dusty masses of Frenchmen launched by Clausel to save the day. In front of them Cole's division reeled backwards towards the Lesser Arapil, while Pack's broken brigade streamed away behind them. Ellis's brigade was pushed back, almost to the Lesser Arapil, while Stubbs's brigade, alongside it, was forced to form a square in order to protect itself from French dragoons who nevertheless got in among some of them. In fact, some French cavalry swept round and got as far as the 6th Division, Wellington's reserve line, which had been brought forward to support the 4th Division.

Clausel's counterattack represented the last, desperate attempt to salvage something from the day's fighting, if not victory itself. But, as so often in his career, Wellington demonstrated his unerring powers of

The steep slopes where Ferey formed his men to cover the retreat of the beaten French army. One can see just how easy it was for the rear ranks of Ferey's men to fire over the heads of those in front. Ferey held out for some time here against Clinton's 6th Division before the arrival of the 5th Division drove him off. Ferey, in fact, was killed here by a round shot.

foresight and at 5.30pm brought forward Clinton's 6th Division, who were fresh and yet to be involved in any of the day's fighting. Clausel's division was attacked not only frontally by Clinton, but also by Spry's Portuguese brigade which Marshal Beresford detached from the 5th Division and led diagonally against Clausel's left flank. Beresford, in fact, was wounded during this attack which halted Clausel's division.

Clinton's 6th Division, meanwhile, continued its advance, with Hinde's brigade on the right and Hulse's on the left, and Rezonde's Portuguese in the second line, their long lines overlapping both ends of Clausel's division. Bonnet's three regiments soon found themselves engaged against a superior firing line and were thrown back upon the main body of Clausel's division, having suffered casualties of around 500 men each. Bonnet's reverse exposed the right flank of Clausel's division and forced it to retreat too. Seizing his opportunity, Wellington directed the 1st Division, still as yet inactive save for the light companies of the Guards, to drive a wedge between Foy and the Greater Arapil, a move which if successful would cut off Foy from the main body of the French army. In the event, Gen. Campbell, commanding the 1st Division, pushed forward only his skirmishers of the King's German Legion, who hardly constituted a real threat to a veteran like Foy. Their advance was, nevertheless, enough to convince the three battalions of the French 120th Regiment, still occupying the summit of the Greater Arapil, that retreat was the better part of valour and they scrambled down the sides of the hill to rejoin the great body of fugitives now streaming away to the south-east, their flank coming under fire from Campbell's Germans as they did so.

With Clausel's courageous counterattack a failure, the battle of Salamanca entered its closing stages. Foy's division was moving slowly but cautiously round the back of the Greater Arapil, threatened all the time by the 1st and Light Divisions; Sarrut's division was heavily engaged

French prisoners being marched back across the Roman bridge over the River Tormes into Salamanca, following the battle on 22 July 1812. After Clark and Dubourg.

trying to stem the relentless advance of the 3rd and 5th Divisions, while Ferey's division clung to the top of a ridge to the south-east of the Greater Arapil. Ferey, in fact, constituted the last line of French resistance as the rest of the French army fell back towards him. Beyond the dark masses of fleeing Frenchmen could be seen clouds of dust through which burst Wellington's triumphant divisions. Away to the west the 3rd and 5th Division drove forward with Bradford's Portuguese and the 7th Division on their left. Squadrons of British and Portuguese cavalry hovered, gathering up surrendering enemy infantrymen and sabring any that resisted. Beyond the Greater Arapil the 1st and Light Divisions advanced, but the main and more immediate threat to the French came from Clinton's advancing 6th Division.

Ferey had been forewarned by Clausel that his division was expected to cover the retreat and the acting commander-in-chief was not to be let down. Ferey was aided considerably by a fairly steep ridge which allowed those at the rear to fire over the heads of those in front, and so more firepower could be brought against the oncoming 6th Division of Wellington's army. Ferey formed seven of his battalions into line with a single square on each flank and when Clinton's men got to within 200 yards of the French position Ferey gave the order to open fire. Scores of dusty red-coated British infantrymen fell as the weight of fire from seven battalions of enemy infantry crashed into them. Clinton's men halted to load and fire and the two sides began a deadly duel of musketry, comparable to that at Albuera, both sides trading volleys for the best part of an hour.

As the light began to fade, the spectacle was made all the more dramatic as the scene was illuminated by scrub fires kindled by burning cartridge papers. The scene itself resembled that at Albuera, and so too did the outcome, for it was the French who eventually broke, the power of Wellington's infantry once again winning the day, but at a price. Indeed, as Ferey's infantry fell back, it was left to the Portuguese to complete the job, the men of the 6th Division having suffered severe casualties. British artillery also joined in to keep Ferey's men on the move and it was a round shot from one of these guns which cut Ferey in two, a sad end for a brave soldier who had inflicted heavy casualties on Clinton's division. Indeed, even with Ferey gone his men continued to put up a gallant fight. They successfully drove back Rezende's Portuguese brigade and it was not until the advancing 5th Division came upon the scene that the final blow was dealt by Wellington's men.

Leith's troops fell upon the left flank of the French, sending the French 70th Regiment into a state of sheer panic. The French army had been making a fighting retreat until that moment, but when the 70th broke and fled, panic spread throughout their ranks and soon almost the whole of the French army was in full flight heading towards the great forest which lay to the south-east of the battlefield. Only the French 31st Light stuck to their task, fighting as they went while chaos reigned all around them. Foy's division fell back in an orderly manner too, shadowed closely by the 1st and Light Divisions, until it too reached the safety of the forest.

The battle of Salamanca ended with Wellington's divisions too exhausted to pursue the French into the dense forest, through which thousands of panic-stricken French troops were fleeing for their lives. There was little point in Wellington sending in what troops he did have available, particularly as he believed that a Spanish force under Carlos d'Espana was holding the only real accessible river crossing over the Tormes at Alba de Tormes. The Spaniards had been left in Alba by Wellington when he had marched north from Salamanca, earlier in the campaign. D'Espana, however, had let his nerves get the better of him, had panicked and had withdrawn his force. Even worse was the fact that he had neglected to inform Wellington of this unauthorised move, rightly fearing the wrath of his commander. Therefore, instead of finding that the remains of the shattered French army were hemmed in against the left bank of the Tormes, an exasperated and furious Wellington discovered that they had simply marched across the bridge and through the fords to make good their escape. Wellington had ordered his divisions north towards Huerta, where the men sank down after the day's exertions.

The battle of Salamanca had been a comparatively short one, but was a most decisive and, for the French, a costly one. Wellington's army suffered some 5,214 casualties, including nearly 700 dead. French casualties are difficult to ascertain, but the historian Sir Charles Oman calculated the number at being around 14,000, including Marmont, Clausel and Bonnet, all of whom had commanded the French army during the day. In addition, 20 guns were taken as well as six colours, which sat rather nicely that evening alongside the two captured eagles.

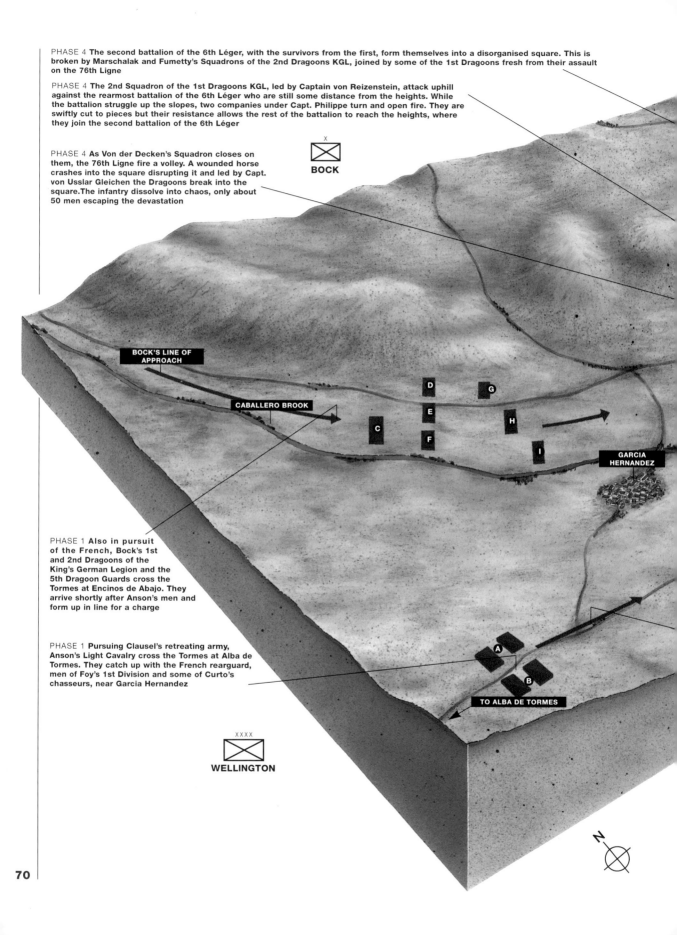

PHASE 4 **The second battalion of the 6th Léger, with the survivors from the first, form themselves into a disorganised square. This is broken by Marschalak and Fumetty's Squadrons of the 2nd Dragoons KGL, joined by some of the 1st Dragoons fresh from their assault on the 76th Ligne**

PHASE 4 **The 2nd Squadron of the 1st Dragoons KGL, led by Captain von Reizenstein, attack uphill against the rearmost battalion of the 6th Léger who are still some distance from the heights. While the battalion struggle up the slopes, two companies under Capt. Philippe turn and open fire. They are swiftly cut to pieces but their resistance allows the rest of the battalion to reach the heights, where they join the second battalion of the 6th Léger**

PHASE 4 **As Von der Decken's Squadron closes on them, the 76th Ligne fire a volley. A wounded horse crashes into the square disrupting it and led by Capt. von Usslar Gleichen the Dragoons break into the square. The infantry dissolve into chaos, only about 50 men escaping the devastation**

X
BOCK

BOCK'S LINE OF APPROACH

CABALLERO BROOK

D

G

E

C

H

F

I

GARCIA HERNANDEZ

PHASE 1 **Also in pursuit of the French, Bock's 1st and 2nd Dragoons of the King's German Legion and the 5th Dragoon Guards cross the Tormes at Encinos de Abajo. They arrive shortly after Anson's men and form up in line for a charge**

PHASE 1 **Pursuing Clausel's retreating army, Anson's Light Cavalry cross the Tormes at Alba de Tormes. They catch up with the French rearguard, men of Foy's 1st Division and some of Curto's chasseurs, near Garcia Hernandez**

A

B

TO ALBA DE TORMES

XXXX
WELLINGTON

N

70

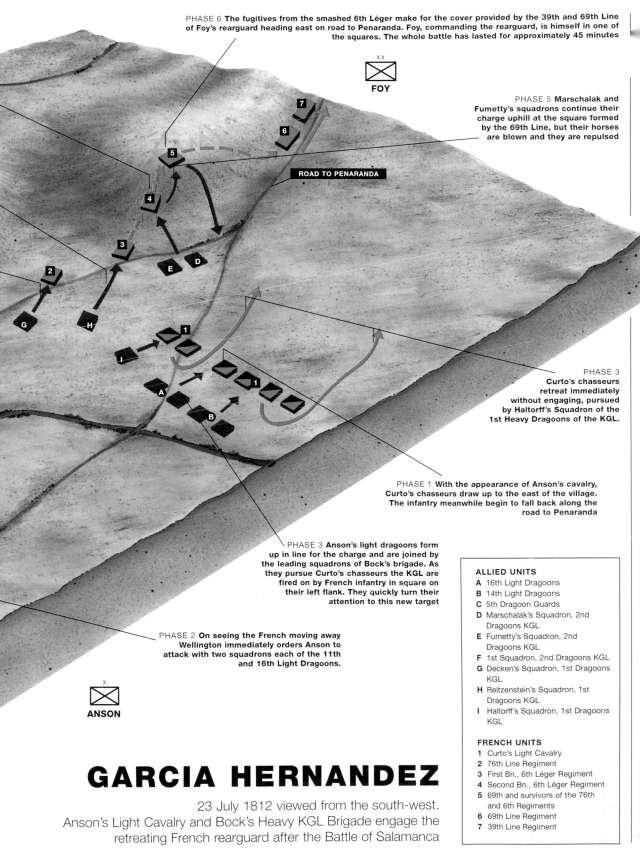

PHASE 6 The fugitives from the smashed 6th Léger make for the cover provided by the 39th and 69th Line of Foy's rearguard heading east on road to Penaranda. Foy, commanding the rearguard, is himself in one of the squares. The whole battle has lasted for approximately 45 minutes

FOY

PHASE 5 Marschalak and Fumetty's squadrons continue their charge uphill at the square formed by the 69th Line, but their horses are blown and they are repulsed

ROAD TO PENARANDA

PHASE 3 Curto's chasseurs retreat immediately without engaging, pursued by Haltorff's Squadron of the 1st Heavy Dragoons of the KGL.

PHASE 1 With the appearance of Anson's cavalry, Curto's chasseurs draw up to the east of the village. The infantry meanwhile begin to fall back along the road to Penaranda

PHASE 3 Anson's light dragoons form up in line for the charge and are joined by the leading squadrons of Bock's brigade. As they pursue Curto's chasseurs the KGL are fired on by French infantry in square on their left flank. They quickly turn their attention to this new target

PHASE 2 On seeing the French moving away Wellington immediately orders Anson to attack with two squadrons each of the 11th and 16th Light Dragoons.

ANSON

GARCIA HERNANDEZ

23 July 1812 viewed from the south-west.
Anson's Light Cavalry and Bock's Heavy KGL Brigade engage the
retreating French rearguard after the Battle of Salamanca

ALLIED UNITS
A 16th Light Dragoons
B 14th Light Dragoons
C 5th Dragoon Guards
D Marschalak's Squadron, 2nd Dragoons KGL
E Fumetty's Squadron, 2nd Dragoons KGL
F 1st Squadron, 2nd Dragoons KGL
G Decken's Squadron, 1st Dragoons KGL
H Reitzenstein's Squadron, 1st Dragoons KGL
I Haltorff's Squadron, 1st Dragoons KGL

FRENCH UNITS
1 Curto's Light Cavalry
2 76th Line Regiment
3 First Bn., 6th Léger Regiment
4 Second Bn., 6th Léger Regiment
5 69th and survivors of the 76th and 6th Regiments
6 69th Line Regiment
7 39th Line Regiment

GARCIA HERNANDEZ

Wellington's cavalry, the King's German Legion excepted, has never really enjoyed a very favourable press as regards its performance in the Peninsula. However, the battle of Salamanca saw the cavalry at its most destructive, with Le Marchant's devastation of the centre of the French army. Yet the battle itself was followed the next day by another demonstration of just what could be accomplished by heavy cavalry in the right circumstances. Indeed, the incident, at Garcia Hernandez has long since been recognised as one of the rare instances of cavalry breaking an enemy infantry square.

The morning of 23 July 1812 found the French army limping away from Salamanca, battered and bruised after its mauling the previous day. Hundreds of French troops were taken prisoner as they wandered round in small groups after becoming separated from the main body of the retreating French army. Wellington, meanwhile, sent Anson's light cavalry in pursuit of the French rearguard, he himself riding with the leading squadrons of light dragoons.

The road to Valladolid had previously been the obvious route for the French army, but after the events of the preceding day this was now out of the question. Indeed, such a course would have taken Clausel's men right across the front of the victorious Allied army. Instead, Clausel's men were retreating to the east, having crossed the Tormes at Alba de Tormes.

Another view of Garcia Hernandez. The village itself lies away to the left, out of shot. Bock's dragoons approached from the left towards the camera, before crossing the road in order to pursue the French rearguard.

The battlefield of Garcia Hernandez. Bock's German dragoons charged from left to right across these fields to achieve its famous demolition of the square of the French 76th Regiment. The French rearguard were trying to gain the heights in the background.

Anson's troops were followed by the 1st and Light Divisions, which had played little part in the victory at Salamanca the day before. Bock's brigade of the King's German Legion, the 1st and 2nd KGL Dragoons were in hot pursuit also, and it was these two latter regiments that were to achieve the remarkable success of 23 July.

Anson's squadrons caught up with the French rearguard at the small village of Garcia Hernandez, on the road to Penaranda. The troops were from Foy's 1st Division which had taken little part in the battle of Salamanca. With them were some of Curto's chasseurs, still smarting after their mauling on the 22nd, as well as a battery of artillery. Upon the appearance of Anson's men the chasseurs drew up just to the east of the village, while the infantry began to draw off along the road to Penaranda. It was these chasseurs that Wellington saw first, with the infantry marching off in the distance. Anson was ordered to attack at once with two squadrons each of the 11th and 16th Light Dragoons.

The King's German Legion Attack

The light dragoons formed up in line for the charge, and were joined shortly after by the leading squadrons of Bock's brigade of the King's German Legion (KGL). Curto's chasseurs turned tail almost immediately and were pursued by the 1st Heavy Dragoons of the KGL. The Germans stood little chance of catching them, but as they rode on they were suddenly struck by a volley which rang out from a body of infantry which had been waiting in square on the Germans' left flank. There were three battalions, in fact, two belonging to the 6th Léger and the other to the 76th Line, altogether numbering about 2,400 men. The volley which had shaken the KGL dragoons came from a square of the 76th, which quickly became the objective of the German cavalry.

The first dragoons to charge against the square of the 76th were from Capt. von der Decken's squadron on the left of the brigade. Decken's men had been hit by the initial volley at a range of about 80 yards. Even at this range quite a few saddles were emptied, but the charge pressed on. The second volley hit the squadron at a much shorter range, about 20 yards. This proved much more devastating, but in an ironic way it proved more damaging to the French themselves. Von der Decken, himself already badly wounded by the first volley, managed to stay in the saddle until the second volley crashed out from the square. Von der Decken's mortally wounded horse rode straight into the square, thrashing and kicking as it did so. The result was a gap, about the space of eight men, into which the heavy dragoons charged, now led by Capt. von Usslar Gleichen, while others leapt the sprawling bodies and began setting about the French with their terrible, long, straight-bladed swords. The whole square was thrown into complete chaos and while scores were hewn down, hundreds of others simply threw down their muskets and surrendered. Only about 50 men escaped the devastation. A single squadron of about 120 men had thus destroyed an entire square of battalion strength.

The other squadrons of heavy dragoons swept past the scene and charged the two battalions of the 6th Léger which were attempting to make for the heights above the road to Penaranda. The second squadron of the 1st Dragoons KGL was commanded by Capt. von Reizenstein who led his men against the rearmost battalion of the 6th Léger, still quite a distance from the heights. While the battalion struggled to the top, two companies of the battalion, under Capt. Philippe, turned about and opened fire on the dragoons. Von Reizenstein's men could not be stopped, however, and they crashed into the two companies, hacking and hewing about them in a frenzied attack. The two companies were quickly dealt with, scores being taken prisoner, but their resistance did allow the rest of the battalion to gain the heights where it joined the second battalion of the 6th Léger which had reached the summit a few minutes before. Here, the two battalions were afforded some protection by a squadron of Curto's chasseurs but, once again, they did not wait to meet the Germans but rode off instead towards the main road, leaving the 6th Léger to its fate.

The 6th quickly got itself into a fairly disorganised square which was totally inadequate to withstand the onslaught of the 2nd Dragoons KGL who were joined by some of the 1st Dragoons, fresh from their assault on the square of the 76th. The heights upon which the 6th Léger formed are significantly higher and it is little wonder that the French commander made for them. It says much for the power and stamina of the KGL cavalry, therefore, that having charged a great distance and having struggled to the summit they were still able to charge home against the ragged square waiting at the top. Indeed, the square dissolved in an instant, hundreds throwing down their muskets while others, more fortunate, took to their heels and made for the cover provided by four battalions of the 39th and 69th Lines which were making off in squares along the road to Penaranda. Foy, commanding the French rearguard, was in one of the squares himself.

The action had lasted some 40 minutes, but in that short space of time one of the most famous attacks of the Napoleonic period had taken place. At a cost of some 127 officers and men killed and wounded out of 700 present, the heavy dragoons of the King's German Legion had inflicted some 1,100 casualties on the retreating French. Many may view the destruction of the 76th's square as sheer luck, given the rather haphazard circumstances that led to it being broken. However, there was nothing lacking in the bravery of the German cavalrymen who made the most of the opportunity when it presented itself. Furthermore, there was no element of fluke attached to the destruction of the battalions of the 6th Ligne. Together with Le Marchant's charge on 22 July, the two days were by far the best enjoyed by Wellington's cavalry in the Peninsula, and probably surpass the achievements of Paget's cavalry at Sahagun and Benavente in 1808 during Moore's retreat to Corunna.

For the remainder of 23 July, and during the 24th, the pursuit of the defeated French army was given over to Anson's cavalry who gathered up scores of prisoners. The main Allied army was too exhausted to make any effective pursuit itself and accordingly, with Clausel's army retreating at great speed, a halt was called at Flores de Avila on 25 July. The campaign of Salamanca was over.

AFTERMATH

With the defeat of Marmont's Army of Portugal, Wellington was left to consider his next move. He could, of course, continue north-east along the great road to France, the French being in no real condition to oppose him for some time. Or he could turn south-east and make for the Spanish capital, Madrid, which offered both political and military advantages. After weighing up the situation Wellington, always acutely aware of the political advantages to be gained from any given situation, decided to march upon Madrid. He entered the capital on 12 August amidst great scenes of celebration by the Spanish people who, after years of French domination, were at last given some cause for optimism.

The year of 1812 had begun with two great strikes against the fortresses of Ciudad Rodrigo and Badajoz, which were taken by the Allies in January and April respectively. These were followed by Hill's triumphant raid on the French bridge and forts at Almaraz in May. The battle of Salamanca continued this victorious trend, culminating in Wellington's advance into

The entry into 12 Madrid by Lord Wellington on August 1812. The clergy, accompanied by several scantily-clad ladies welcome the great man into their city. His staff can be seen at right.

The battle of Vittoria, 21 June 1813. Wellington's victory here crushed forever all French hopes of being able to cling on in the Peninsula. The battle was the most decisive of the war and saw the main French field army thrown back across the Pyrenees into France.

Madrid. And yet, the year ended disastrously and disappointingly for Wellington, with his army back on the Portuguese border around Ciudad Rodrigo. The crushing victory of Salamanca had, in the words of Gen. Foy, raised Wellington's standing throughout Europe to that of Marlborough's, and had nailed for good Wellington's reputation of being a purely defensive-minded commander. However, it was the failure of Wellington's army to conduct proper siege operations that was to return to haunt him and bring about the only real disaster of the war for him, the retreat from Burgos in October and November 1812.

After the occupation of Madrid, Wellington headed north-east with a portion of his army to lay siege to the castle of Burgos, perched high on a hill overlooking the town itself. Wellington undertook the siege woefully short of siege matériel: he had only three heavy guns with him, totally insufficient for the operation. Also, he had none of his 'storming' divisions with him, but instead relied on the 1st Division of the army which, having been denied the opportunity to take part in any of the earlier stormings or of the fighting at Salamanca, had begged to be allowed to take part in the operation against Burgos. Sadly, the 1st Division was not up to the job and only the Brigade of Foot Guards came out of the operation with any credit. The siege wore on throughout September and October with little success, culminating with the death of Edward Cocks, one of Wellington's favourite officers, who died repulsing a French sortie. On 21 October Wellington's men began to withdraw from the town and so began the disastrous retreat from Burgos which was accompanied by all the miseries of the retreat to Corunna in the winter of 1808-09. In fact, those who endured both miserable episodes later declared that the retreat from Burgos was by far the worse.

Once again, the commissariat broke down, men starved and took to looting what few Spanish habitations could be found along the sparsely inhabited plain. Torquemada, one such town, was the centre of the region's wine-producing area and, unfortunately, was stocked with the year's recently gathered wine stocks. Needless to say, Wellington's men needed no invitation to fall out and gorge themselves on the vast liquid feast to be found in the town's vaults and cellars. Hundreds of drunken soldiers were rounded up by the French when they entered the town afterwards. The retreat ended with Wellington's army concentrated around Ciudad Rodrigo where Wellington issued his infamous memorandum concerning the conduct of his officers during the retreat.

By the spring of 1813 the army had recovered, and with rein-

SIX MONTHS OF MIXED FORTUNES 1812

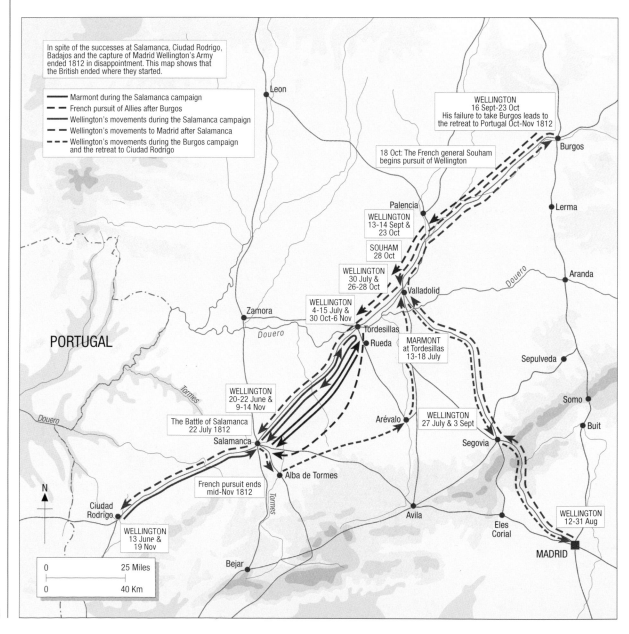

In spite of the successes at Salamanca, Ciudad Rodrigo, Badajos and the capture of Madrid Wellington's Army ended 1812 in disappointment. This map shows that the British ended where they started.

— Marmont during the Salamanca campaign
-- French pursuit of Allies after Burgos
— Wellington's movements during the Salamanca campaign
— Wellington's movements to Madrid after Salamanca
-- Wellington's movements during the Burgos campaign and the retreat to Ciudad Rodrigo

WELLINGTON
16 Sept-23 Oct
His failure to take Burgos leads to the retreat to Portugal Oct-Nov 1812

18 Oct: The French general Souham begins pursuit of Wellington

Leon

Burgos

Lerma

Palencia

WELLINGTON
13-14 Sept &
23 Oct

SOUHAM
28 Oct

Aranda

WELLINGTON
30 July &
26-28 Oct

Valladolid

WELLINGTON
4-15 July &
30 Oct-6 Nov

Zamora

Douero

Tordesillas

Rueda

MARMONT
at Tordesillas
13-18 July

Sepulveda

PORTUGAL

Douero

WELLINGTON
20-22 June &
9-14 Nov

Somo

Buit

Tormes

The Battle of Salamanca
22 July 1812

Arévalo

WELLINGTON
27 July & 3 Sept

Salamanca

Segovia

Douero

French pursuit ends
mid-Nov 1812

Alba de Tormes

Tormes

N

Ciudad
Rodrigo

WELLINGTON
13 June &
19 Nov

Avila

Eles
Corial

WELLINGTON
12-31 Aug

MADRID

0   25 Miles

0   40 Km

Bejar

The 14th Light Dragoons in action towards the end of the battle of Vittoria. The regiment became known as 'The Emperor's Chambermaids' after they 'acquired' Joseph's chamber pot. An astonishing amount of loot was plundered by the British and Portuguese troops after the battle from the French baggage train which was loaded to the full with treasure accumulated over years of French occupation. (After a painting by Hillingford)

forcements from England Wellington was ready to begin his advance once more into Spain. The advance began on 20 May 1813, a moment of some poignancy for Wellington who turned in his saddle and exclaimed, 'Farewell Portugal, for I shall never see thee again.' He never did.

The advancing columns of Wellington's army converged at Vitoria where, on 21 June, they crushed the army of Joseph Bonaparte and effectively ended any hopes that might have lingered in the minds of the French that they would be able to remain in Spain for much longer. The French were driven over the Pyrenees, leaving just the army of Suchet,

The crossing of the Bidassoa, 7 October 1813. British hussars and infantry cross the Bidassoa to set foot on the 'sacred soil' of Napoleon's France. This superb painting by James Beadle also shows Royal Horse Artillery to the left and a Spanish guide, behind the cavalryman in the centre. Fuenterrabia lies on the southern bank of the river in the background.

The sortie from Bayonne, 14 April 1814. The sortie was launched against the blockading Allied forces days after hostilities had ended. The governor of Bayonne, Thouvenot, refused to go quietly, however, and some 1,500 casualties on both sides was the price of his mischievousness.

fighting on the eastern coast of Spain, south of the border. Napoleon replaced Joseph with Marshal Soult who set about restoring the shattered confidence of the French army before mounting a counterattack across the Pyrenees on 25-30 July. The attack failed, however, and Wellington's army was left poised to cross the Bidassoa and set foot on French soil which they did on 7 October. The following month the Allies drove the French from their positions along the line of the River Nivelle, flushing them from the rocky crags of the Greater Rhone and from their redoubts which ran from St Jean de Luz as far as the Mondarrain Mountain. The year ended with Wellington's army encamped to the south of the Adour at Bayonne. Here, on 9 December, Soult launched yet another counterattack, momentarily driving the Allies back during four days of heavy and confused fighting astride the River Nive. Once again, however, the attack failed. Soult withdrew, leaving Bayonne to its fate while he headed east towards Toulouse.

Wellington, meanwhile, spent the winter at St Jean de Luz, planning his next operation, the crossing of the Adour. This hazardous crossing took place on 14 February 1814 and resulted in the total isolation of Bayonne. A covering force was left behind to blockade the town, while Wellington's main field army set off in pursuit of Soult. The two armies clashed at Orthes on 27 February, yet another victory for Wellington. There were numerous other skirmishes along the road to Toulouse, notably at Tarbes and Aire, before the final battle of the war, at Toulouse itself on 12 April 1814. This bloody encounter need never have taken place, however, as Napoleon had abdicated on 6 April. Despite this, on 14 April Thouvenot, the governor of Bayonne, launched a sortie which left some 1,700 combatants either dead, wounded or taken prisoner after some bloody night-fighting

In the words of one of the great historians of the Peninsular War, Sir William Napier, Bayonne 'thus terminated the war, and with it all remembrances of the veterans services.' The great Peninsular army was dismantled and divided between America, Britain and other overseas stations. And yet there was still one more great battle for some of Wellington's men, namely Waterloo, but the army that fought there under the great Duke was a pale shadow of that which had triumphed in Portugal, Spain and southern France, and which had swept Marmont's army from the field of Salamanca.

THE BATTLEFIELD TODAY

The battlefield at Salamanca is one of the more unspoilt battlefields of the Peninsular War. Indeed Wellington would recognise it in an instant were he alive today. It is situated some 6km south of Salamanca and is centred on the small village of Los Arapiles. This sprawling village was held by the Light Companies of the Coldstream and 3rd Foot Guards, and although the French secured a footing on the outskirts, it remained in Allied hands throughout the day. The two most dominant features are, of course, the Arapiles, two peculiar-shaped hills that appear to have been dropped on the plain from heaven. It is quite an easy climb to the top of the Lesser Arapil, which was held by Wellington's men during the battle, and from here one can gaze out to the north, behind the hill, and picture the two armies as they took up their initial positions running north–south.

The small chapel at the edge of the French position is still standing. Across the valley stands the Greater Arapil, which was occupied by Marmont during the battle, and away to the west of the Lesser Arapil is the village of Los Arapiles itself, with the San Miguel Hill behind it. It was from this hill that Wellington watched the opening stages of the battle. Looking further west from Lesser Arapil, across the main road south from Salamanca, is the village of Miranda de Azan, which is now 1km west of the main road. It is best to begin any tour of the battlefield from here, because this is where Packenham's 3rd Division struck Thomières' troops. It is possible to follow Packenham's route along a track south from Aldea de Tejada all the way to Miranda, although the woods which hid his division from the French have long gone. The slopes up which the 3rd Division marched are still free of any building, even today.

From Miranda travel back to Los Arapiles and take a track south out of the village to the slope up which Leith's 5th Division advanced to attack. From the top you can look down on the valley below and imagine Maucune's division with Clausel's division on its right, and visualise Le Marchant's cavalry charging from the rear of Los Arapiles. From here go back to the village, turn right - to the east - and make for the Greater Arapil. This is a steeper climb than the Lesser Arapil, but from the top one can see all the way to Salamanca itself, and the area where Wellington's divisions

The obelisk on top of the Greater Arapil on the battlefield at Salamanca. It has been cleaned up recently and its base strengthened.

The valley to the east of the two Arapiles. The French troops advanced south behind the ridge in the distance. Foy's troops remained there throughout the day watched by the 1st and Light Divisions which were away to the left.

formed up. It also puts paid to the myth that Marmont could not see behind Wellington's front line. He certainly would not have been able to see Pakenham's advance, but even on a grey day it is possible to see most of the ground behind Los Arapiles. Looking directly west from the Greater Arapil, it is easy to follow the attacks made by Leith and Le Marchant, and to appreciate just how far the fugitives from Thomières' routed division would have had to come in order to retreat to the woods to the south-east of the battlefield. It is easy to follow the attack of Cole's 4th Division, whose battalions advanced from between the Lesser Arapil and the village of Los Arapiles. A small stream marks to within a few yards the position of Stubbs's brigade as it attacked. As Cole advanced, Pack threw his Portuguese brigade forward in support, up the slopes of the Greater Arapil, which remain unchanged. The steep ledge which caused them to put down their muskets in order to climb it, is easy to find.

Wellington's victory was secured by Clinton's 6th Division advancing from behind the San Miguel Hill. Away to the south-east lie the woods where the French retreated. The wood has thinned, but only slightly, and the rocky ridge which allowed Ferey's men to fire over the heads of their comrades in front is clearly visible.

With a few extra days it is possible to follow the campaign all the way from Tordesillas to Los Arapiles, and on to Garcia Hernandez. Wellington's position on 20 June at San Cristobal is clear, and it is easy to find the sites of the fights close to the villages of Castrejon and Canizal. The course of the celebrated parallel march can be traced with good maps, as can the fords over the Tormes. Traces of the Salamanca forts also remain. The old bridge at Alba de Tormes, where Wellington had hoped to ensnare Marmont's army, still stands. Further east lies Garcia Hernandez, which is dominated by the heights of La Serna. There are three obvious defiles, all with roads running over them, so it is difficult to pinpoint the exact point at which Foy's squares were broken by the charge of Bock's dragoons.

Five days are really necessary to study this fascinating campaign thoroughly, although the area of the main battlefield can be tackled in just one day. Accommodation is plentiful in Salamanca, where there is a parador as well as several other hotels.

THE PENINSULAR WAR: CHRONOLOGY

1807

18 October	French troops cross the Spanish frontier.
30 November	Junot occupies Lisbon.

1808

23 March	The French occupy Madrid.
2 May	Uprising in Madrid.
14 July	The French, under Bessières, defeat the Spaniards, under Cuesta and Blake, at Medina del Rio Seco.
22 July	The French, under Dupont, surrender at Baylen.
1 August	A British force, under Sir Arthur Wellesley, lands at Mondego Bay, Portugal.
17 August	Wellesley defeats Delaborde at Roliça.
21 August	Wellesley defeats Junot at Vimeiro.
30 August	Convention of Cintra: Wellesley recalled to England.
30 October	The French evacuate Portugal.
8 November	Napoleon enters Spain with 200,000 men.
4 December	Napoleon occupies Madrid.
December	Moore advances from Salamanca.
21 December	British cavalry victory at Sahagun.

1809

16 January	Moore killed at Battle of Corunna.
22 April	Wellesley returns to Portugal.
12 May	Wellesley crosses the Douro and captures Oporto.
28-29 July	Wellesley defeats Joseph at Talavera.
4 September	Wellesley is created Viscount Wellington.

1810

10 July	Massena takes Ciudad Rodrigo.
24 July	Craufurd defeated by Ney on the Coa River.
27 September	Wellington victorious over Massena at Busaco.
10 October	Wellington enters the Lines of Torres Vedras.
14 October	Massena discovers Lines and halts.
17 November	Massena withdraws to Santarem.

1811

5 March	Graham victorious at Barrosa.
10 March	Soult takes Badajoz.
3-5 May	Wellington defeats Massena at Fuentes de Oñoro.
6 May	Beresford begins first British siege of Badajoz.
11 May	Brennier abandons Almeida to Wellington.
16 May	Beresford defeats Soult at Albuera.
19 May -17 June	Second British siege of Badajoz.

1812

8 January	Siege of Ciudad Rodrigo begins.
19 January	Wellington takes Ciudad Rodrigo by storm.
6-7 April	Wellington takes Badajoz by storm.
22 July	Wellington defeats Marmont at Salamanca.
12 August	Wellington enters Madrid.
19 September	Wellington begins siege of Burgos.
22 October	Wellington abandons siege of Burgos.
22 Oct.-19 Nov.	Allied retreat to Portugal.
19 November	Allied army arrives at Ciudad Rodrigo.

1813

21 June	Wellington defeats Joseph at Vitoria, created Field Marshal.
25 July	Soult makes counterattack in the Pyrenees. Battles at Maya and Roncesvalles.
28-30 July	Wellington defeats Soult at Sorauren.
31 August	Graham takes San Sebastian by storm.
31 August	Soult repulsed at San Marcial.
7 October	Wellington crosses the Bidassoa into France.
25 October	Pamplona surrenders.
10 November	Wellington defeats Soult at the Battle of the Nivelle.
9-12 December	Wellington defeats Soult at the Battle of the Nive.
13 December	Soult repulsed by Hill at St Pierre.

1814

27 February	Wellington defeats Soult at Orthes.
6 April	Napoleon abdicates.
10 April	Wellington defeats Soult at Toulouse.
14 April	French sortie from Bayonne.
17 April	Soult surrenders.
27 April	Bayonne surrenders.
30 April	Treaty of Paris.
3 May	Wellington created Duke.

ORDER OF BATTLE

WELLINGTON'S ARMY AT SALAMANCA

CAVALRY

Le Marchant's Brigade: 3rd Dragoons, 4th Dragoons, 5th Dragoon Guards
Anson's Brigade: 11th Light Dragoons, 12th Light Dragoons, 16th Light Dragoons
V. Alten's Brigade: 14th Light Dragoons, 1st Hussars KGL
Bock's Brigade: 1st and 2nd Dragoons KGL

INFANTRY

1ST DIVISION, H. Campbell
Fermor's Brigade: 1/Coldstream, 1/3rd Guards, 1 coy. 5/60th
Von Lowe's Brigade: 1st, 2nd and 5th Line Bns. KGL.
Wheatley's Brigade: 2/24th, 1/42nd, 2/58th, 1/79th and 1 coy. 5/60th

3RD DIVISION, E. Pakenham
Wallace's Brigade: 1/45th, 74th, 1/88th, 3 coys. 5/60th
Campbell's Brigade: 1/5th, 2/5th, 2/83rd and 94th

4TH DIVISION, L. Cole
Anson's Brigade: 3/27th, 1/40th and 1 coy. 5/60th
Ellis's Brigade: 1/7th, 1/23rd, 1/48th and 1 coy. Brunswick Oels

5TH DIVISION, J. Leith
Greville's Brigade: 3/1st, 1/9th, 1/38th, 2/38th and 1 coy. Brunswick Oels
Pringle's Brigade: 1/4th, 2/4th, 2/30th, 2/44th, 1 coy. Brunswick Oels

6TH DIVISION, H. Clinton
Hulse's Brigade: 1/11th, 2/53rd, 1/61st and 1 coy. 5/60th
Hinde's Brigade: 2nd, 1/32nd and 1/36th

7TH DIVISION, J. Hope
Halkett's Brigade: 1st Light, 2nd Light, KGL. and remainder Brunswick Oels
De Bernewitz's Brigade: 51st, 68th, and Chasseurs Britanniques

LIGHT DIVISION, C. Alten
Barnard's Brigade: 1/43rd coys. of 2/95th, 3/95th and 1st Caçadores
Vandeleur's Brigade: 1/52nd, 1/95th and 3rd Caçadores

ARTILLERY

Royal Horse Artillery
Ross's Troop, Macdonald's Troop and Bull's Troop
Field Artillery
Lawson's, Gardiner's, Greene's, Douglas's and May's companies
KGL Artillery
Sympher's Battery

PORTUGUESE CAVALRY

D'Urban's Brigade: 1st and 11th Portuguese Dragoons

PORTUGUESE INFANTRY BRIGADES

Pack's Brigade: 1st Line (2 Bns.), 16th Line (2 Bns.), 4th Caçadores
Bradford's Brigade: 13th Line (2 Bns.), 14th Line (2 Bns.), 5th Caçadores
Power's Portuguese Brigade: 9th Line (2 Bns.), 21st Line (2 Bns.),
   12th Caçadores
Stubbs's Portuguese Brigade: 11th Line (2 Bns.), 23rd Line (2 Bns.), 7th
   Caçadores
Spry's Portuguese Brigade: 3rd Line (2 Bns.), 15th Line (2 Bns.)
   8th Caçadores
Rezende's Portuguese Brigade: 8th Line (2 Bns.), 12th Line (2 Bns.), 9th
   Caçadores
Collins's Portuguese Brigade: 7th Line (2 Bns.), 19th Line (2 Bns.),
   2nd Caçadores

PORTUGUESE ARTILLERY

SPANISH TROOPS

Carlos de España's Division: 2nd of Princesa, Tiradores de Castilla, 2nd of Jaen, 3rd of 1st Seville, Caçadores de Castilla, Lanceros de Castilla.

British Troop Numbers

Infantry	25,577
Cavalry	3,553
Artillery	1,186
Engineers	21
Staff Corps	86
Train	139
TOTAL	**30,562**

Portuguese Troop Numbers

Infantry	17,421
Cavalry	482
Artillery	114
TOTAL	**18,017**
Spanish Troops	3,360
TOTAL	**51,939**

THE ARMY OF PORTUGAL

1ST DIVISION, Foy
Brigade Chemineau: 6th Léger (2 Bns.), 69th Ligne (2 Bns.)
Brigade Desgraviers-Berthelot: 39th Ligne (2 Bns.), 76th Ligne (2 Bns.)
Artillery Train, etc.

2ND DIVISION, Clausel
Brigade Berlier: 25th Léger (3 Bns.), 27th Ligne (2 Bns.)
Brigade Barbot: 50th Ligne (2 Bns.), 59th Ligne (2 Bns.)
Artillery Train, etc.

3RD DIVISION, Ferey
Brigade Menne: 31st Léger (2 Bns.), 26th Ligne (2 Bns.)
Brigade (unknown): 47th Ligne (3 Bns.), 70th Ligne (2 Bns.)
Artillery Train, etc.

4TH DIVISION, Sarrut
Brigade Fririon: 2nd Léger (3 Bns.), 36th Ligne (3 Bns.)

Brigade (unknown): 4th Léger (3 Bns.), 130th Ligne (absent)
Artillery Train, etc.

5TH DIVISION, Maucune
Brigade Arnaud: 15th Ligne (3 Bns.), 66th Ligne (3 Bns.)
Brigade Montfort: 82nd Ligne (2 Bns.), 86th Ligne (2 Bns.)
Artillery Train, etc.

6TH DIVISION, Brennier
Brigade Taupin: 17th Léger (2 Bns.), 65th Ligne (2 Bns.)
Brigade (unknown): 22nd Ligne (3 Bns.), Régiment de Prusse (remnant of)
Artillery Train, etc.

7TH DIVISION, Thomières
Brigade Bonté: 1st Ligne (3 Bns.), 62nd Ligne (2 Bns.)
Brigade (unknown): 23rd Léger (absent), 101st Ligne (3 Bns.)
Artillery Train, etc.

8TH DIVISION, Bonnet
Brigade Gautier: 118th Ligne (3 Bns.), 119th Ligne (3 Bns.)
Brigade (unknown): 120th Ligne (3 Bns.), 122nd Ligne (3 Bns.)
Artillery Train, etc.

LIGHT CAVALRY DIVISION, Curto
3rd Hussars (3 Squadrons)
22nd Chasseurs (2 Squadrons)
26th Chasseurs (2 Squadrons)
28th Chasseurs (1 Squadron)
13th Chasseurs (5 Squadrons)
14th Chasseurs (4 Squadrons)
Escadron de Marche

HEAVY CAVALRY DIVISION, Boyer
6th Dragoons (2 Squadrons)
11th Dragoons (2 Squadrons)
15th Dragoons (2 Squadrons)
25th Dragoons (2 Squadrons)
Artillery attached to cavalry

Artillery Reserve	1,500
Engineers and Sappers	349
Gendarmerie	135
Equipages militaires	768
État-Major-Général	54

French Troop Numbers

Infantry	43,266
Cavalry	3,575
Auxiliary Arms	2,806
TOTAL	**49,647**
Guns	78

A GUIDE TO FURTHER READING

There is a vast array of literature on the Peninsular War, including general histories, specialist studies, regimental histories and memoirs and diaries. The most obvious ports of call when embarking upon any study of the war are the three works by Fortescue, Oman and Napier. The latter was an eye-witness to many of the events and his six-volume history has become a classic. It also inspired - and influenced - many of the veterans who subsequently put pen to paper and published their own accounts of their experiences in the Peninsula. The definitive work on the Peninsular War, however, remains Oman's great seven-volume history which is unlikely to be surpassed. Both of these great multi-volume histories have been reprinted in recent years, unlike Fortescue's momentous *History of the British Army*, which, being all of thirteen volumes in length, not to mention the additional atlas volumes, is unlikely to be reprinted. Fortescue's work spans many centuries of the army's history before petering out towards the end of the Victorian era. The Peninsular War consumes no less than five volumes, from 6 to 10, and is at the very core of his work. Probably the finest single-volume work on the Peninsular War is the late Jack Weller's *Wellington in the Peninsular* which, although treating the conflict from a purely British – and Wellingtonian – standpoint is a superb study, covering both military and topographical aspects of the war.

As regards single works on the Salamanca campaign itself, there are very few. By far the best study is Marindin's *The Salamanca Campaign*, published in 1906. Unfortunately, it is a fairly rare beast and does not appear too often in the hallowed pages of antiquarian booksellers. Lawford and Young's *Wellington's Masterpiece* is another good campaign history, although a substantial part of the book is taken up with the events leading up to the battle, such as the stormings of Ciudad Rodrigo and Badajoz, and Hill's attack on Almaraz. Nevertheless, it is fairly easy to obtain and in spite of some poor battlefield photographs - some of which look as if they were taken from the vibrating cockpit of a WW2 fighter plane – and some amateurish, although helpful, sketches, it is a useful book to get hold of.

Wellington's own account of the campaign can be found, as usual, amongst the pages of Gurwood's *Despatches*, whilst scores of participants left us their own accounts of the battle, which are, however, too numerous to list here. The nine works listed below are just a few of the many books on the Peninsular War and Wellington's army, most of which contain their own bibliographies which will help the reader find his way through the mass of literature available.

Fletcher, Ian, *Wellington's Regiments*, Staplehurst, 1994.
Fortescue, The Hon. J.W., *History of the British Army, Vol. 8*, London, 1917.

Gurwood, J, *Despatches of Field Marshal the Duke of Wellington, Vol. 9,* London, 1838.

Haythornthwaite, Philip J., *Wellington's Military Machine,* Tunbridge Wells, 1989.

Lawford, J.R., & Young, P,. *Wellington's Masterpiece,* London, 1972.

Marindin, Captain Arthur Henry, *The Salamanca Campaign,* London 1906.

Napier, Sir William. *History of the War in the Peninsula, Vol.5.* London, 1836.

Oman, Sir Charles, *A History of the Peninsular War, Vol. 5.* Oxford, 1914.

Weller, Jack, *Wellington in the Peninsula,* London, 1962.

Another view from the Lesser Arapil. The village of Les Arapiles is on the right. The 4th Division advanced between the hill and the village.

INDEX

PLACES TO VISIT

Touring the Salamanca and Ciudad Rodrigo Sites

If a visit to Salamanca is planned it makes sense to extend the tour to include Ciudad Rodrigo and the sites of battles and skirmishes on the border with Portugal. They lie some 100 km (60 miles) apart. The following text is aimed at helping those planning a visit of their own. The alternative is to make the journey with a suitably qualified guide such as the author of this book. Ian Fletcher Battlefield Tours may be contacted at P O Box 112, Rochester, Kent ME1 2EX, UK. Tel [44] (0)1634 319973. Fax [44] (0)1634 324263. E-mail: enquiries@ifbt.co.uk, website: www.ifbt.co.uk

Books useful to the independent traveller are:

Paget, Julian, *Wellington's Peninsular War: Battles and Battlefields*, London, 1990. It has succinct text and clear battlefield plans.

Robertson, Ian C., *Wellington at War in the Peninsula 1808-1814 - An Overview and Guide*, Barnsley, 2000. Narrative text, road maps, battle plans and numerous illustrations, plus tourist information.

Of interest is:

Fletcher, Ian, and Andy Cook, *Fields of Fire*, Staplehurst, 1994. Evocative photographs with military appreciation of terrain.

Tourist information may be had from www.tourspain.es and from the following Spanish Tourist Offices:

Australia: Suite 144, 303 Castlereagh Street, Sydney, NSW 2000.
Tel: 612 264 7966.
Canada: 2 Bloor Street West 34th Floor, M4W 3E2 Toronto.
Tel: 416 961 3131.
United Kingdom: 22-23 Manchester Square, London W1M 5AP.
Tel: 0207 486 8077. Website: www.tourspain.co.uk
United States of America: 666 Fifth Avenue (Floor 35), New York,
NY 10103. Tel: 212 265 8822.
In Spain:
Regional Tourist Offices, Castilla y Leon:
37008 Salamanca, Casa de las Conchas, Compañia, 2.
Tel: [34] (923) 26 85 71. Fax: 26 24 92.
37500 Ciudad Rodrigo, Arco de las Amayuelas, 6.
Tel: [34] (923) 46 05 61.
Municipal Tourist Office:
37002 Salamanca, Plaza Mayor, 10. Tel: [34] (923) 21 83 42.

Visitors should remember that extremes of weather were experienced by the combatants and may likewise torment the modern traveller. Spring and autumn are the least risky seasons. Ciudad Rodrigo is at an altitude in excess of 500m (1640ft) and the climate is therefore that much less warm than its latitude suggests. The terrain can be rough for those exploring on foot and drivers without 4-wheel-drive, high-axle vehicles may be more limited in their investigations than they might like.

Drivers should familiarize themselves with Spanish regulations and a visit to the website of the DGT, the responsible authority in Madrid, is wise. On www.dgt.es an English language text is available for the Highway Code and other information. The Autoroutes in Spain are toll-free in the case of 'N' roads, while some quite heavy tolls are levied on the 'A' roads. Cash payment is needed. Leaded fuel comes as *Super* or *Normal*, unleaded is *Sin Plomo* and diesel is labelled *Gasoleo*. LPG gas is available only to public service vehicles. Credit cards can be used at fuel stations on principal roads, but cash may be needed off the main through-routes.

Hotels, including the perfectly acceptable though less luxurious *Hostales*, and camp-sites are listed in regional leaflets available from the Tourist Offices. Top of the list for comfort and reliability are the *Paradores*, the four-star state-run hotels.

While in touch with the Tourist Office be sure to obtain the leaflets with general tourist and cultural information. There are many wonderful things to see, experience and to eat and drink, so do not miss the chance to enjoy the country.

The Border Sites

(Michelin map 940 refers. Detailed coverage of events associated with these sites can be found in Ian Fletcher's *Badajoz 1812*, Osprey Publishing.)

The Battle of Fuentes de Oñoro, 3–5 May 1811

The main road, now the E80 and the IP5 in Portugal, the E620 in Spain, from Guarda to Ciudad Rodrigo crosses the border near Fuentes de Oñoro. In spring 1811 Wellington had his headquarters at Freineda, to the west, and was besieging Almeida, to the north. Fort Conception lies between the rivers Turones (in Portugal) and Dos Casas (in Spain), south-west of Aldea del Obispo. In spite of being blown up by the British on 21 July 1810, more than enough survives to justify a visit.

On 3 May the French, under Masséna, undertook a frontal attack at Fuentes, crossing the river but ending the day back where they had started. A truce on the 4th allowed both sides to gather in their dead and wounded. Wellington anticipated an attack on his right, southern, flank the next day and strengthened his line at Poço Velho and Nave de Haver. The open country favoured the French with their numerical superiority of cavalry and, on 5 May, they began to fold up the British and Portuguese line from the south. Wellington succeeded in reforming his line west to east, north of the road through Fuentes to Freineda, while Craufurd's Light Division covered the retreat of the rest of the line northwards. Against these fresh dispositions the French failed. Masséna ordered the garrison at Almeida (well worth visiting; a complete fortified town) to withdraw and, to Wellington's discomfiture, they succeeded in escaping north-eastwards during the night of 10 May.

From the main road east of the Dos Casas River the old road of 1811 can be seen and the advantage of Wellington's position on 5 May is clear.

The Action at Barba del Puerco, 19 March 1810

A spectacular Roman bridge spans the River Aqueda near San Felices de los Gallegos, north-west of Ciudad Rodrigo. It was on the delicate line held by the British and guarded by Craufurd's Light Division. On the night of 19 March the French attacked and overcame the piquets on the bridge and on the road, but the shooting aroused their comrades of the 95th Rifles from their sleep in the village above and, in their nightclothes and shirtsleeves, they turned out to fight desperately and successfully to throw back the aggressors.

Craufurd's Coa River Defence, 24 July 1810

West of Fuentes de Oñoro the autoroute bridge overshadows the old bridge over which Craufurd was slow to retreat, endangering his 52nd Light Infantry. Only the swift intervention of officers of the 43rd Light Infantry and the 95th Rifles saved them. The continuing attacks of the French failed.

The Siege of Ciudad Rodrigo, 8–19 January 1812

Wellington planned in 1811 to capture Ciudad Rodrigo early in 1812 and he put the town's siege in the hands of Julian Sanchez and his Spanish guerrillas. The British arrived by 7 January. The town was vulnerable; first, because it was, with only 2,000 men, under-garrisoned and, second, because it was overlooked from the north by two parallel ridges, the Great Teson some 650 metres away and the Little Teson about 180 metres from the walls. Fort Reynard on the former was taken on the night of 8 January by 300 picked men of the Light Division. The long, cold, slow work of digging parallels – approach trenches – and battery positions began the next day. By 13 January the heavy siege guns were in position and the convent of Santa Cruz, south west of the Little Teson, had been taken. The French gave Wellington a set-back the next morning by making a sortie and in the afternoon it was found that the siege guns needed to be resited. However, by the evening of 18 January two breaches had been made. At 1900 hours on 19 January, in moonlight, Major-General Robert Craufurd led his Light Division forward. Once they entered the ditch the French fiercely opened fire on them and as they gained the breach and prepared to clear the ramparts to the north, Craufurd fell. He died on 23 January.

On the west Lieutenant Colonel O'Toole, with Portuguese and British troops, crossed the Roman bridge and dealt with the guns at the castle. From Santa Cruz the 5th and 77th Regiments forced their way into the ditch and made for the Greater Breach. Major-General Henry Mackinnon arrived with his brigade as the breach was being entered. At that moment the French blew a great mine, killing and wounding many of their own men as well as their enemies – including Mackinnon. Two guns to the left rear of the breach continued the French resistance until the gunners were bayonetted and the British poured into the town. British casualties were 9 officers killed and 70 wounded and 186 men killed and 846 wounded. The French lost 8 officers killed and 21 wounded and about 500 men killed and wounded, while 60 officers and 1,300 men were made prisoner and the siege train was taken.

The fortified town survives without excessive intrusion of modern industry or building. The E80/N620 now by-passes the town to the south, leaving the area of interest on the northern side relatively peaceful (see photograph opposite).

The old town of Ciudad Rodrigo is well preserved and it is possible to walk a complete circuit of the walls. Enter by way of the tunnel in the eastern wall, the site of the Lesser Breach stormed by the Light Division. Immediately within, on the right, is a memorial plaque to Craufurd. From the ramparts one can look towards the convent of San Francisco along the approach route of the Light Division and then walk north towards the site of the Great Breach. The cathedral is passed, and on it signs of artillery damage can be seen. From the site of the Great Breach the importance of the Great Teson can be appreciated in spite of the blocks of flats now built on the Little Teson. A walk to the central plaza allows the imagination to picture the marauding British pouring into the dark town. Continue to the old Moorish Castle, now an hotel, to see the importance of its location

This aerial photograph shows the town as seen from the north. The site of the Great Breach was in the angle of the walls at the bottom left and the site of the Lesser Breach is halfway up the left side, the east, where a road enters the town and where a tower stood in 1812. At the extreme right, the west, is the Castle below which the 5th entered the ditch. The importance of silencing the guns in the castle enclosure, from which the 5th would have been enfiladed, is evident. The river Agueda flows at top right.

and the route over the Roman bridge taken by O'Toole. The guns his men neutralized were in what is now the hotel garden.

The Battle of Salamanca, 22 July 1812
(Michelin map 444 refers.)
Some 80km, just over 50 miles, to the north-east of Ciudad Rodrigo, the British and Portuguese fought the first battle of the advance into Spain after Badajoz and Ciudad Rodrigo had been secured. The E80/N620 runs from Ciudad Rodrigo to Salamaca and will, or now does, form a by-pass to the south of the town. The battle itself centered on the village of Los Arapiles, some 6km to the south of Salamanca by the N630 (and a turn to the east), and it is by the name of the village that the French and Spanish know it.

The author's advice for visiting the battlefield is on page 81. The manoeuvres leading up to the battle are shown on the map on page 34 and a drive 34km north-east on N620 brings you to Cañizal, Wellington's position of 18 July. A minor road to the south-east leads to the valley of the river Guarena across which the English and French observed each other (see pages 30 to 32). The movements of the armies on 21 and 22 July are shown on the map on page 42. The modern N630 passes between Ian Fletcher's suggested start point (see page 81), Miranda de Azan (bottom left of the map) and Los Arapiles (north-east of Miranda). The positions of the Lesser and Greater Arapils, east of Los Arapiles, can be seen on that map as well. The text on pages 81 and 82 suggests the best way to appreciate the battle from these hills, and the photographs on pages 56 to 61 will assist, as will the bird's-eye views on pages 38-39 and 54-55. The river crossing at Alba de Tormes is where the modern C510 from Salamanca goes. To the east is Garcia Hernandez, or Garcihernández as it is known today, (see pages 70-71 and 82).

In England

The National Army Museum
Location: Royal Hospital Road, Chelsea, London
Tel: 0207 730 0717. Open daily 10am to 5.30pm
The museum tells the story of the British Army from 1485, when the

Yeoman of the Guard were raised, to the present day, and the Peninsular War is thus part of the coverage.

Apsley House
Location: Hyde Park Corner, London. Tel: 0207 499 5676
Open Tuesday to Sunday and Bank Holidays, 11am to 5pm
This is the former residence of the Duke of Wellington and the paintings, sculpture, furniture and porcelain are proof of the esteem in which he was held throughout Europe (except, presumably, by certain persons in France). The house is a branch of the Victoria and Albert Museum.

Wellington Exhibition, Stratfield Saye House
Location: Stratfield Saye, south of Reading, Berkshire, by A33
Tel: 01256 882882. Open May to September daily except Friday
The exhibition contains personal memorabilia of the Duke, books once the property of Napoleon and the grave of Wellington's horse, Copenhagen.

Essex Regiment Museum
Location: Chelmsford and Essex Museum, Oaklands Park, Moulsham Street, Chelmsford, Essex. Tel: 01245 353066
The museum covers the service of the 44th (East Essex) and 56th (West Essex) regiments from 1741 to 1881. The exhibits relating to the Peninsular War include the eagle taken at Salamanca.

As so many British units served in the Peninsula regimental museums throughout the country have items relating to the war. See: Marix Evans, Martin, *The Military Heritage of Britain and Ireland*, London, 1998.

COMPANION SERIES FROM OSPREY

MEN-AT-ARMS
An unrivalled source of information on the organisation, uniforms and equipment of the world's fighting men, past and present. The series covers hundreds of subjects spanning 5,000 years of history. Each 48-page book includes concise texts packed with specific information, some 40 photos, maps and diagrams, and eight colour plates of uniformed figures.

ELITE
Detailed information on the uniforms and insignia of the world's most famous military forces. Each 64-page book contains some 50 photographs and diagrams, and 12 pages of full-colour artwork.

NEW VANGUARD
Comprehensive histories of the design, development and operational use of the world's armoured vehicles and artillery. Each 48-page book contains eight pages of full-colour artwork including a detailed cutaway.

WARRIOR
Definitive analysis of the armour, weapons, tactics and motivation of the fighting men of history. Each 64-page book contains cutaways and exploded artwork of the warrior's weapons and armour.

ORDER OF BATTLE
The most detailed information ever published on the units which fought history's great battles. Each 96-page book contains comprehensive organisation diagrams supported by ultra-detailed colour maps. Each title also includes a large fold-out base map.

AIRCRAFT OF THE ACES
Focuses exclusively on the elite pilots of major air campaigns, and includes unique interviews with surviving aces sourced specifically for each volume. Each 96-page volume contains up to 40 specially commissioned artworks, unit listings, new scale plans and the best archival photography available.

COMBAT AIRCRAFT
Technical information from the world's leading aviation writers on the aircraft types flown. Each 96-page volume contains up to 40 specially commissioned artworks, unit listings, new scale plans and the best archival photography available.